Managerial Communication for Organizational Development

Managerial Communication for Organizational Development

Reginald L. Bell
Jeanette S. Martin

 BUSINESS EXPERT PRESS

Managerial Communication for Organizational Development
Copyright © Business Expert Press, LLC, 2019.

First published in 2019 by
Business Expert Press, LLC
222 East 46th Street, New York, NY 10017
www.businessexpertpress.com

ISBN- 978-1-94784-331-8
ISBN- 978-1-94784-332-5

Business Expert Press Corporate Communication Collection

Collection ISSN: 2156-8162 (print)
Collection ISSN: 2156-8170 (electronic)

Cover and interior design by S4Carlisle Publishing Services Private Ltd., Chennai, India

First edition: 2019

10 9 8 7 6 5 4 3 2 1

Printed in the United States of America.

Dedication

To our spouses, immediate family members, and students:
Our heartfelt thanks to our families for allowing
unfettered time on weekends to work on
the book and for your patient support.
We are grateful to our students for their input
on ideas and topics that were necessary
inclusions for this second edition.

—Reginald and Jeanette

Abstract

Managerial Communication for Organizational Development offers a functions approach to managerial communication as well as explores what the communication managers actually do in business across the planning, organizing, leading, and controlling functions. The Windows into Practical Reality add contemporary information pertinent to key concepts in the chapters. Focusing on theory and application that will help managers and future managers understand the practices of management communication, this book combines ideas from industry experts, popular culture, news events, and academic articles and books written by leading scholars. The chapters will help any manager realize the full capacity of its organizational objectives, both internally and externally. Organizational development is the relationships built by effective managerial communication.

All of the levels of communication (intrapersonal, interpersonal, group, organizational, and intercultural) play a role in managerial communication and are discussed thoroughly. The top, middle, and frontline communications in which managers engage are also addressed. Expounding on theories of communication, the authors relate them to the theories of management—such as organizational culture and climate, equity theory, leadership and power, technology in communication, communication process model, ethics, and conflict resolution. These are the knowledges that are invaluable to management.

Keywords

change; climate; coaching; commitment; conflict resolution; corporate social responsibilities; culture; customer service; cyber theft; delegation; empowerment/engagement; equity theory; ethics; expectancy theory; feedback; financial reporting; hierarchies; incivility; leadership; negotiating; organizational development; performance; scientific management; social justice warrior; stakeholders; strategic planning/career development; teams; technical core; technology; training/workplace learning; trust; value chain

Contents

Preface

Purpose

Managerial Communication for Organizational Development offers a unique functions approach to managerial communication. Readers will be engaged by a focus on theory and application that will help managers and future managers understand the practices of management communication. *Managerial Communication for Organizational Development* combines ideas from industry experts, popular culture, news events, and academic articles and books written by leading scholars. It merges popular communication theories with broadly accepted management theories to provide practical solutions to managerial problems that occur across the functional areas and tiers of management. After reading *Managerial Communication for Organizational Development* managers will have a much better insight about how to handle a plethora of business problems confronting today's manager.

Contents

The book includes six chapters emphasizing the essentials of managerial communications for top, middle, and frontline managers engaged in the four functional areas of planning, organizing, leading, and controlling.

The book is especially useful for managers and mid-career working adults enrolled in MBA programs, as there are many examples to which they can relate. The materials will also serve as guideposts for professors doing research and teaching in the managerial communications field. Professors with little or no industry experience will find the chapters' contents replete with workplace examples. Professionals and future managers will find the contents of the book engaging and refreshing due to the real-world approach. Currently, there is a gap between academic research and business practice linking managerial problems to communications solutions. This book sheds light on particular techniques of management communication as they are used by people engaged in managing others at each level of the organization and across the various functional areas.

Managerial Communication for Organizational Development

Instructor's Manual

PowerPoint (PPT) slides for each chapter are included, which highlight the concepts of each chapter. The PPT is accessible from Business Expert Press by request from persons who will use the book for teaching purposes. In addition, the test questions are also available from Business Expert Press. Test items include structured-response and essay items. Questions and cases assessing mental abilities at the higher levels of the cognitive domain (analysis, synthesis, and evaluation levels) are emphasized.

Reginald L. Bell, PhD

Jeanette S. Martin, EdD

Acknowledgments

Thanks to Our Editor

We appreciate the honest and accurate feedback received from Debbie DuFrene, our editor, who helped us tremendously with our book. The features, figures, tables, charts, and graphs were all made much better because of Debbie's meaningful comments; her untiring efforts were essential in shaping this book. We appreciate her surgical pen and feel that her insistence on points of view, technical details, and painstaking adherence to specificity has made this book a useful tool in preparing professionals to resolve management problems that require well-developed communication skills. She ensured that balance was adhered to with the presentation of representative views on both sides of controversial issues, especially in the Windows into Practical Reality features in each chapter. We also appreciate the efforts of others who reviewed the book's chapters and materials.

CHAPTER 1

The Nature of Managerial Communication

Objectives

After reading this chapter, you will be able to:

1. explain how management and communication form managerial communication;
2. explain how managers use managerial communication to motivate;
3. explain the need for communication policies;
4. identify the processes of group or team communication in traditional and virtual environments.

Introduction

Your success as a manager depends on your ability to communicate effectively. In today's global economy, that is not easy because technology is producing more information, complicating the way in which people from different countries and cultures communicate, as well as how they communicate with people with various business specialties. The ability to sift through the information, cultures, and disciplines is time-consuming, and the amount of information being processed is but one of many existing barriers to communication. This book is a guidepost through those barriers that will help you focus your managerial communication (MC) to make your organization as efficient as possible.

As a manager, you need strong communication competency to work with diverse groups of people in an ever-changing global work world. It takes a great deal of skill to both manage and communicate well. Understanding how the disciplines of management and communication have come together to form MC will help you understand the importance of MC in the organization.

Origins of Managerial Communication

When people think of *management*, they think of it as something people do in an organization to get things done. *Management* is the "act or art of managing: the conducting or supervising of something (as a business)" or "the judicious use of a means to accomplish an end" (Merriam-Webster's online 2014). When people think of *communication*, they think of message exchanges between a source and a receiver. The basic definition of *communication* is "to make commonly understood." Therefore, MC is the use of management and communication skills to make information commonly understood in order to accomplish organizational goals.

The fields of management and communication continue to evolve through scientific investigation. The two fields were a fledgling collection of ideas in the 1900s. Compared with the more ancient fields, such as philosophy or mathematics, management and communication are still infant fields of study. However, management and communication have advanced through scientific investigation.

Management

The management theories we use today have developed over time. Management scholars talk about four managerial functions, and textbooks define *management* generically as the process of planning, organizing, leading, and controlling to achieve the stated goals by using resources judiciously. The field of management employs the classical approaches, which include perspectives on scientific management principles, administrative management, bureaucratic management, behaviorism, human relations, and so on. Contemporary approaches include perspectives on quality circles, organizational behavior, quantitative analysis, and contingency theories. The classical perspective, a more pessimistic managerial view, pioneered  by Frederick W. Taylor shown in the photo at the bottom left of this page, is often referred to as Theory X, where managers felt their subordinates had nothing to offer the company except their manual labors. The behavioral perspective, a more optimistic managerial view, is referred to as Theory Y, where managers began to realize that the workers could be a source of assistance if encouraged to do so. The human relations perspective, put forth by William Ouchi and referred to as Theory Z, involved the quality circle approach to managing, teaching American businesses to adapt to the art of Japanese management styles. Theory Z focused on increasing employee loyalty to the company by providing a job for life with a strong focus on the well-being  of the employee, both on and off the job. According to Ouchi (1981), Theory Z management tends to promote stable employment, high productivity, and high employee morale and satisfaction through his examination of the evolving culture of "Z" people in society. Management scholars agree that contributions by people such as Max Weber, Henri Fayol (shown in the photo at the top right of this page), Frederick W. Taylor, Chester I. Barnard, Joan Woodward, Mary Parker Follett, Herbert Simon (shown in the photo at the bottom right of this paragraph), Elton Mayo, and W. Edwards Deming helped to shape the field of management. In fact, their books are considered by many to be the most influential management books of the twentieth century (Bedeian and Wren 2001). Frederick W. Taylor's work revolutionized early American industrial organizations, leading to the scientific management approach. Elton Mayo's and Fritz Roethlisberger's work at the Hawthorne plant in Illinois is largely responsible for shaping managers' understanding of the direct effect that social interaction has on productivity in the workforce, thus ushering in the human relations movement. Edward Deming's research on quality circles and teams further revolutionized management theory. The field of management evolved largely from the ideas of these people.

Communication

Communication studies grew out of the field of management studies. The National Communication Association defines communication as "a group of instructional programs that focus on how messages in various media are produced, used, and interpreted within and across different

contexts, channels, and cultures, and that prepare individuals to apply communication knowledge and skills professionally" (Morreale and Backlund 2002, p. 7). Peter F. Drucker (1954), shown in the photo at the top left of this page, argued that management was the effective use of motivation and communication, one of five basic tasks of the manager.

Moreover, it was in the 1950s that communication studies began to concentrate on an individual's relations with other individuals (Morreale and Backlund 2002). Along with management studies, communication studies revealed evidence that workers could help improve operations when their ideas were considered. Communication

studies became more relationship oriented. Mary Parker Follett (shown in the photo at the left) was a management philosopher, whose contributions helped business leaders recognize the importance of effective communication of human beings within the organization. What is clear about her emphasis on motivation and interpersonal communication skills is that they are predicated on effective management. She is also credited with offering the following sage advice: "Management is the art of getting things done through people." Follett's writings are featured with commentary in the 1995 Harvard Business School Press book, *Follett: Prophet of Management.*

As the study of the fields of management and communication evolved concurrently, practitioners became increasingly aware that communication is an essential competency for managers and their subordinates.

Managerial Communication

Management and communications theories go hand in hand at all levels of the organization: top, middle, and frontline. Morreale, Rubin, and Jones (1998) listed the study of relationship management as part of interpersonal and group communication skills. Managers must control conflict, allow others to express different views, know how to effectively be assertive, analyze situations, and exchange information. Managers who practice these skills successfully are effective communicators. The role of effective MC in the workplace is to help the firm succeed.

The Role of Managerial Communication

Managers play many complex roles in the workplace: mind reader, detective, analyst, pundit, and fortune-teller. But managers are only human, and they need two-way communication to truly know what is happening in their work worlds. A manager's worst communication error is to assume that everyone has and understands the information that has been conveyed. On the flip side, as any help wanted advertisement will prove, a manager's most important competence—and the one most executives look for in college graduates—is the ability to communicate. Using writing, speaking, listening, and nonverbal skills effectively to translate organizational ideas into productive worker actions contributes directly to a healthy bottom line.

A successful communication is a message that is understood in the way that the sender intended and leaves the sender and receiver on good terms. These criteria for successful communication are consistent with Barnard's (1968) views on coordinated systems of organizational control and the most important function of the executive (Zuboff 1988). In this role, managers ensure the downward, horizontal, and upward exchange of information, and transmission of meaning through informal or formal channels that enable the achievement of the goal (Bell and Martin 2008).

Effective MC is imperative to achieving the mission of any company, and no manager can succeed in the classic management functions of planning, organizing, leading, and controlling without it. By communicating effectively at all levels—top, middle, and on the front line, as well as across internal boundaries and interculturally—a manager can help the organization exert a positive influence on the community in which it is located and be as profitable as possible for its owners.

In the late 1980s and early 1990s, communication theorists wrote articles that defined the boundaries of several professional disciplines in the field of communication (Shelby 1993). For the purposes of scientific investigation in professional communication, the discipline is often divided into four areas: organizational, business, corporate, and MCs. These areas are not exactly mutually exclusive (managers can be engaged in two or more of these types of communication simultaneously), but they are distinct enough to be considered separate disciplines within the field.

Four Types of Workplace Communication

Organizational communication is the study of how in a complex, system-oriented environment people send and receive information within the organization, and the effect that it has on organizational structure. The type of communication focused on at the organizational level would include improving coordinated systems of control.

Business communication focuses on studying the basic use of both written and oral skills. For example, business communication focuses on developing the fundamental concepts of written communication principles, such as grammar, unity, emphasis, coherence, construction of standard documents used in a business environment—that is, bad news and good news messages—progress reports, reprimands, and job search skills such as resumes and employment application letters. Business communication overlaps with managerial and corporate communication in that these documents are what form the history of the corporation.

Corporate communication focuses on creating a desired world reputation and image of the organization. For example, the duties of a director of corporate communications would include the task of overseeing the writing of the company's external documents such as the annual report.

MC merges business communication, organizational communication, corporate communication, and management. Figure 1.1 illustrates how management and the other three areas of communication are interdependent, with MC emerging as the main communication in the workplace.

MC combines the management and communication theories in the workplace to help managers function as planners, organizers, leaders, and controllers of a company's limited resources in order to achieve the stated goals. In fact, it is impossible for any manager to function without MC at any level of management. Take a moment and try to plan, organize, lead, or control a project without using communication on some level.

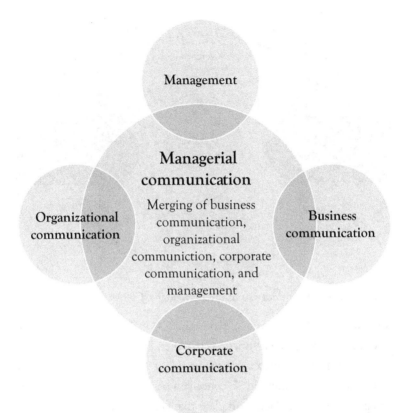

Figure 1.1 Managerial communication overlap

Communicate to Motivate

Figure 1.2 illustrates the Communicate to Motivate Model (CMM) and its constituent parts. *Planning* sets up a blueprint for future actions needed to achieve agreed-upon goals. *Organizing* determines who will do what and why. *Leading* occurs when top managers share their vision of the future and then shape organizational culture to achieve that vision. *Controlling* systematically gauges the organization's actual performance against the established plans and goals and calibrates adjustments in areas of weakness.

Along with resources, managers use their functions to attain the goals of the organization. Imagine trying to accomplish any of these functions without goal-directed communication. Froschheiser (2008) argues that business leaders need to preach "communication, communication, communication" (p. 9). Every employee should know the company's goals.

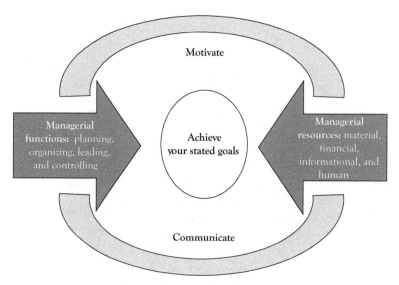

Figure 1.2 Communicate to motivate model—CMM

No confusion. No exceptions. Communication is the "golden thread" tying all the management functions together. For example, you can conceive of a brilliant plan; however, successful interpersonal communication is necessary to implement it. To conceive a plan is to communicate on an intrapersonal level. In fact, most plans that failed did so somewhere in the communication process.

Geneen, a former ITT executive, wrote that to "manage means to get something done, to accomplish something that you, or the team of managers, set out to do, which presumably is worthy of your effort" (Geneen and Moscow 1984, p. 105). What is implicit in all the earlier definitions is that managers work for owners, especially in profit-seeking enterprises. Managers successfully operate businesses for owners to achieve their goals, so as to dominate the market as the number one recognized brand. Whether owners bear the risk of failure or enjoy the safety of success, employees will expect them to provide the resources for them to do their jobs. Thus, we could say that the real work of a manager is to help owners judiciously utilize resources to accomplish the owners' goals. (Nonprofit organizations may have benefactors and donors instead of owners, while government organizations have stakeholders such as voters and tax payers.) This managerial task requires motivating and communicating with employees.

Employees are the organization's most important resource because only human resources can be developed and improved in a way that makes them more productive (Drucker 1954). No nonhuman resource is capable of being the boss! Therefore, managers must always strive to continually improve their ability to motivate their employees. In management terms, motivating an employee means getting him or her to do a good job independently with little help.

Motivation can be done with a stick (threat, punishment) or with a carrot (incentive, reward). The carrot approach is preferred for building an organization of employees who take initiative and are proactive in helping achieve the stated goals. Employees work better when rewarded for good work. Because motivation is a large part of the leadership function, motivation theories are nearly always included in the prominent part of management textbooks. Window into Practical Reality 1.1 shows a good example of a manager getting things done through people using her interpersonal communication skills.

Window into Practical Reality 1.1

Getting Things Done Through People

George Stanford and his wife Jennifer worked in different careers for 25 years, George as an accountant and Jennifer as a manager for several large retail discount chains. They had two children, Lucinda and Ryan, 19 and 17, respectively. Though things were going well for the couple, Jennifer was not content with her career and decided to do something about it. George and Jennifer agreed that they would take the plunge and use $200,000 of their retirement and other savings, nearly a third of their total assets, to purchase a restaurant franchise. They decided on a gourmet burger and fries established chain that showed good bottom-line numbers and a rapid rate of return in a short time.

Things went well in the first year, with sales revenues exceeding $1.5 million and netting the couple $180,000 in before taxes income. However, the second year, Jennifer, who agreed to put full-time effort into the business, noticed that the revenues had started to decline 30 percent and that none of the factors that would suggest a decline in revenues were present, such as foot traffic or major competition emerging in the immediate surrounding metropolitan area. The products she ordered through the franchisor had not declined in quality either. Jennifer, having read a bit while completing her bachelor's degree in management from a major university in the Phoenix area, remembered Mary Parker Follett as an exemplar in management theory, who had recognized that a key to getting people to do the things you would have them do is keeping them motivated.

What did Jennifer do to solve her problem?

Jennifer knew that she could not directly ask her employees questions about their behavior because they would give her a *socially desirable response*. In other words, they would tell her what they thought she wanted to hear. Jennifer also suspected that unmotivated employees were the cause of her rapidly diminishing bottom line. She therefore hired a few people from her church whom she trusted to visit her establishment randomly for about a month. Their responses did not surprise her. However, she was a bit disappointed that some of the long-term employees did not appear to respect the customers, deliberately mistook orders, and were a bit rude to the loyal customers who frequented the place. Using the reports from the spies, Jennifer was able to verify this unprofessional employee behavior by viewing the surveillance videos at those times.

Rather than terminating the employment of the long-term employees, who had earlier been very loyal to her franchise, Jennifer created an incentive plan that would motivate them to do the right thing, whether she was in the restaurant or not. She used her interpersonal communication skills by asking each employee individually and privately about his or her goals and aspirations for the future. Once she learned about these things, she integrated her employees' aspirations with her incentives program. Some employees needed more immediate things, such as a better car or more money for child-care expenses. These employees were motivated to behave in a way that would make them eligible to receive monetary bonuses, up to $1,000 annually. Others were motivated to earn points, making them eligible for the new George & Jennifer Stanford Scholarship assistance program that could contribute up to $2,500 a year toward an employee's college tuition. She then retrained all her employees on upselling techniques, courteousness, and respect for customers. They knew clearly now what Jennifer expected them to do, and they knew that Jennifer knew what they wanted from her.

Needless to say, with feedback from the people doing the work and integrating their needs and desires into the incentives for doing good productive work, Jennifer was able to stave off disaster and recover the revenues she had lost in the previous year.

Jennifer figured out how to help her frontline employees plan and control the amount of their paychecks by doing something extra, such as upselling to customers (suggesting other items on the menu prior to closing the sale). She learned that few of her employees saw their jobs with her franchise as a career; thus, she used their own ambitions as a means to an end. For her employees who were enrolled in college, she was able to make college more affordable, as long as they treated her business and customers as they should be treated, with respect and courteousness.

Although managers must build a strong working relationship with employees, this should not be confused with building friendships, because that is not the goal of effective communication. A manager needs to do his or her job without bias or favoritism. Holding back constructive criticism on the basis of friendship is a sign of a weak manager.

Motivating a football player on a pro-team or motivating a food worker at McDonald's is accomplished by communicating with the employees what is expected of them; what their position does for the firm, the team, the customer, and for the employee; and by using positive reinforcement—praising an employee for a job well done, or passing along a thank you for caring about the customer. The manager is motivating the employee and molding the employee into the type of team player the manager wants in order to have a successful organization. Since many of us watch collegiate or professional sports, or eat at fast-food restaurants, we can quickly identify the teams that seem to run like a machine and the ones that are very disjointed. Sports fans may avoid watching their favorite team play when they are not winning. While lack of talent could be to blame, the problem also could be that they are not being motivated properly and are not being communicated with in such a way that they are motivated to win. Likewise, most people have their favorite fast-food restaurants that they revisit because of the service. A manager builds employee customer service skills and the loyalty of the customer through effective planning, organizing, leading, and controlling.

Managerial Communication by Management Tier

We can use MC theories to explain communication responsibility across the three tiers of management (top, middle, and frontline). Figure 1.3 shows who starts the communications process and who carries out the directions. At the strategic level, top management deals with conceptual problems and direction-setting for the organization. At the tactical level, middle managers direct the human elements of the organization. At the operational level, the frontline managers use their technical skills on behalf of the organization.

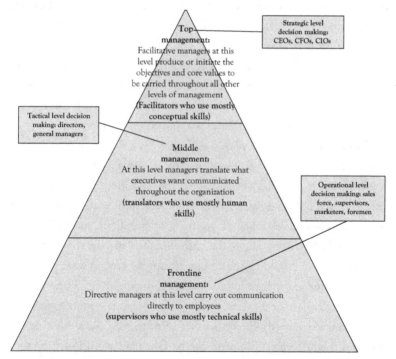

Figure 1.3 Managerial communication decision making by tier

While in theory the tiers make sense, the study by Harcourt, Richerson, and Wattier (1991) of 871 U.S. middle managers' communication practices showed information to be moving in and through middle managers as opposed to out from them. The middle managers did not always communicate the information that was pertinent to the subordinates. In addition, Brownell (1990) provides evidence of middle managers' listening skills and how they rated themselves as listeners in the hospitality industry. While they rated themselves as good listeners, their subordinates did not. Lawler, Porter, and Tennenbaum (1968) surveyed 105 managers who evaluated themselves to be higher on self-initiated interactions than non-managers and subordinates. A different study found that 105 managers evaluated self-initiated interactions with other managers higher than those initiated by subordinates or nonmanagers. As the studies show, most managers have a lot of work to do in using communication to motivate and help subordinates do their jobs.

Information changes as it progresses through levels of management; therefore, the accuracy of information should always be questioned. Channels will be discussed in the next chapter, a subject that is important to show how top management communicates goals throughout the company.

One typical leading or motivating function of frontline management is reprimanding an employee who is tardy. Most frontline managers will follow a prescribed system of progressive disciplinary actions—verbal warning, first written warning, second written warning, and dismissal—to reinforce compliance and gain commitment (Frankel and Otazo 1992). What different kinds of communication could result? To what degree does an employee's frequency of communication with an immediate supervisor change pre- and postreprimand? Does the employee openly complain about the supervisor, regardless of whether the reprimand was fair and accurate? Does his or her productivity change? How does the supervisor's choice of words affect employee behavior in the short and long term? Answers to testable questions like these add to the resources that management research can provide to practitioners. All of these questions are important.

After a frontline manager has reprimanded an employee, the most important question is: "What to do in order to motivate the employee again after the reprimand?" A reprimand should not cause an employee to lose his or her motivation. In fact, Taylor, Fieldman, and Lahlou (2005) found that blood pressure was significantly higher when recipients were reading a threateningly worded reprimand when compared with a nonthreateningly worded reprimand.

In the past, MC was oriented more toward practicing managers who needed to understand communication theory from a more pragmatic perspective than toward the development of the basic skills, which are normally the focus of business communication. Therefore, a background in management principles and basic communication skills developed in an undergraduate business communication course are helpful to the manager.

Communication competency is the use by a manager of a combination of knowledge, skill, behaviors, and attitudes. If a manager expects to make good decisions, he or she must understand the structure of the organization. The manager must be able to plan the goals within the organization for which he or she is responsible. The manager must then lead teams to perform tasks that will reach the stated goals of the organization and the subunit.

Finally, the manager must have a way to evaluate the performance and correct any shortcomings. One way of doing this is to develop a routine that includes frequent, in-depth discussions about performance with employees. Asking specific questions to help the employee along can be important. Such questions might include: What have you accomplished? How did you measure accomplishments? What do you want to accomplish in the next few months? What measurements might you use for those accomplishments? What has to be done? And, how can I help?

Being a great manager at any level requires competency in many areas: communication, planning and administration, teamwork, strategic action, global awareness, and self-management. Communication competency includes informal and formal communication and the ability to negotiate. Planning and administration competency involves the ability to gather information, analyze it, and develop a solution to a problem. It also includes the ability to use time management, to be able to plan and organize multiple projects, and to do so within the budget.

Teamwork competency involves the ability to design an appropriate team, to motivate team members and support them with a creative environment, and to manage the dynamics of the team that will develop. Strategic action competency is understanding the environment in which you work, including not only your organization but also the industry as a whole, before you take a strategic position and put it into action. Global awareness competency is being knowledgeable about other cultures with whom you work, understanding differences, and being open to discussions when cultural misunderstandings arise. Self-management competency includes your personal integrity and ethical beliefs, drive, resilience, self-awareness, personal development, and the ability to balance work and life issues (Hellriegel, Jackson, and Slocum 2007).

Picture managerial communicators as rational planners, decision makers, and commanders; they often work in harried environments switching in a few minutes from one person or problem to another. Many times the environment is anything but quiet. Finding the time to plan and thoughtfully consider every communication does not always happen as a manager would like. Being successful in the business world and in your career will not happen without good communication skills. Learn as much as possible about strategies that have been successful, identify your own weaknesses, and then work to correct them. If you are an extrovert, you may talk too much and need to learn to listen more. If you are an introvert, you may be a good listener but need to learn to talk more and to assume a greater leadership role in guiding people. Try out some of the other suggestions in this book to see if they work for you.

A major problem in business today is information overload. You will have to determine which messages require your time and which ones simply contain "nice to know" information that can be filed or deleted entirely. Becoming a user of information yourself and repackaging this information for others takes a great deal of time and communication. Communication policies help members of an organization understand to whom they should be communicating and when. For example, medication has benefits, but also has side effects, especially for a long-time user. A wealth of information creates a poverty of attention. That is why we must be selective when receiving and sharing information.

Communication Policies

How organizations use communication is somewhat individualized; all companies have an organizational culture and climate. While you may not find an organization's communication policies in published form, the culture of the firm reveals those policies. The culture and communication within the organization reflect the beliefs, values, and attitudes of the organization. The *organizational climate* is the environmental quality that the workers experience. Climates can be very supportive, defensive, positive, or negative. Generally, a supportive climate begins at the top with leaders who are nonjudgmental, open to ideas, trusting, and believe in participatory decision making. If you work in an organization where everyone works overtime, then you will probably feel that you should also work overtime. The culture and climate of the organization drive the organization's communication style and unconsciously control the motivation to communicate.

Communication drives organizational culture, too. IBM began using a program called *JAMS* to allow employees to discuss ideas. With this program, a data-mining program can be used to analyze discussions for themes. This facilitates very open discussions because *JAMS* participants join, exit, and rejoin ongoing discussions and very quickly see where the discussion is going as they reenter an existing discussion. Moderators (those who lead and facilitate focus groups) can also sort out themes that emerge (Spangler, Kreulen, and Newswanger 2006).

Many organizations have had communication policies or a communication manual in place for a long time. Normally, the policies integrate the mission statement and goals of the firm within the communication function. Important policy items include a crisis communication plan, public relations communication, human resources communication policies, norms for treating proprietary information, communications etiquette, and the appropriate channels (formal documents, e-mail, blogging, social media, and so on) for the different kinds of information disseminated. The fact remains that many companies do not take the time to build a policy book until something negative happens as in the example shown in the Window into Practical Reality 1.2.

Window into Practical Reality 1.2

Using Social Media as a Communication Tool

U.S. President Donald Trump utilizes Twitter constantly. Some say it is too much, and others say they like it because they are getting messages directly from him without media interpretation. The mainstream media cannot twist his words when people can read the message for themselves. However, this is a change from past presidents who always went through channels and whose comments were more controlled. Social media has changed our society in many ways. How a company's employees use social media should be part of the organization's employment manual.

While communication policies may not work all the time, they can be helpful in addressing questions about the correct way to communicate certain kinds of information. For instance, organizations are governed by laws as well as company policy concerning what a company representative can say about an employee. The media often makes public statements that are said as an aside or in confidence. It would be easy for a member of the press or the market competition to overhear a salesman talking on the phone in a public area of the airport. Employees must be aware of when and where they can talk about company business. Firms often allow only certain people to discuss company information outside the company office building. If employees have a problem, you want them to come to someone within the company with their grievance and not go to the press. Having employees sign a general confidentiality statement and explaining what the statement means is one way of making this message clear.

Communicating in Teams

Managers generally bring people together to solve a problem; they assign a task and let the team work independently until they have a solution. Prior to the 1970s, formal communication was the standard approach in most businesses. The team-based management approach in the late 1970s moved firms from very formal to more informal communication. In this approach, teams participate more fully in company decision making through less formal communication channels and are highly involved with coordination between the functional teams they represent. They not only solve problems but also develop relationships between the functional areas of the company by supporting one another.

How do teams use formal and informal communication channels? First, it is necessary to define the term *team*. A *work team* is typically made up of a small number of people; they should have complementary skills, should share the common purpose of the team, should have the freedom to set their goals, and should require very little direct supervision. Effective teams also have the ability to solve problems, resolve conflict internally, distribute leadership among the team members, and evaluate their processes. Essential soft skills include understanding the feelings and needs of coworkers, communicating effectively, and dealing with any barriers that may appear. Teams can be formal or informal. *Formal teams* are often appointed to carry out ongoing work assignments on a permanent basis. *Informal teams* are a casual coming together of people to work on an informal basis throughout the organization. It is important to have different talents and specialties within a team, as for instance when introducing a new product. In this case, the team should be cross-functional, comprised of people from different areas of the organization who can apply their varied expertise to the project.

Successful teams demonstrate emotional intelligence, quality interaction, and distributed leadership. Studies have shown that as a result of successful team interaction, workers are happier and empowered, efficiency increases, there is synergy between departments, and the lines of communication are more open. With people from different departments talking directly with each other, layers of management are eliminated, thereby increasing efficiency. The company is able to draw upon the skills, imagination, and creativity of the whole workforce for problem solving and developing new ideas.

A team must maintain good communication. Achieving the task assigned, maintaining the social morale of the team, and helping each member of the team to grow are essential to success. Effective teams must develop trust, make sure that everyone understands their role in the team, and discuss shared goals and expectations. Such interactions aid in the development of synergy (a combined greater value of multiple ideas versus one person working on a project) among the members and distributed leadership. These team processes require open communication and strong verbal, nonverbal, and visual communication skills. Team members who lack good interpersonal communication skills jeopardize the success of the team. Team members should feel comfortable expressing concerns, and a healthy discussion should follow. Basically, team members train one another on how they can communicate as a team. Effective teamwork can enhance communication within the company as well as with customers and business partners, as redundancies can be eliminated.

Phases of Team Development

Effective teams move in rather predictable ways through a series of phases as they blend their experiences, talents, and skills to complete their assigned task. Initial team assessment involves assessing the performance and characteristics of all members individually, looking at how they fit in with the team, institution, culture, and technology as well as their skills in analyzing, documenting, implementing, and evaluating each other (Yarbrough 2003). It is important for the team to know what their strengths and weaknesses are as individuals and as a team. There needs to be a climate of trust if members are to honestly share their information. This exercise also helps members of the team, who do not know one other, to get to know one another as individuals and teammates.

- After completing the initial assessments, the team enters *Phase 1* of team development, which is setting out roles and responsibilities. Time spent here will help the performance of the team later. Some of the things that should be done in *Phase 1* include deciding who will be the communication hub manager and being sure everyone has the needed information. Members also need to decide on a team manager who will be responsible for procedures, tasks, and assignments. One member should be responsible for all documents and the dissemination of those documents, and someone needs to maintain the database or website with accurate information for the team to access and use. The climate manager helps to maintain good relationships between team members and ensure full participation, and the conflict manager helps to reduce any conflicts that arise between team members. In small teams, individual members may perform more than one of these discussed roles.

- *Phase 2* involves managing the procedures that have been set in place. During this phase the team members will negotiate and come to a consensus on the task and its subparts.
- *Phase 3* involves performing or finalizing tasks, training, updates, meetings, and reporting to the appropriate constituents.
- *Phase 4* involves reporting to management, and the team's evaluation of their performance. It is good for teams to celebrate successes.

Celebration could involve going to lunch together, having a drink after work, or something else. Generally, when you are part of a team, it is in addition to your normal job, which means that it is extra work. Taking time to celebrate and receiving recognition from management makes it easier to do the work and will help the team perform well in the future. Making use of the great power of friendship can strengthen the team. Effective teams tend to be self-motivated but can also fall into "groupthink."

Groupthink happens when a team stops generating new ideas, suppresses critical thinking, and squelches divergent thought. The best way to avoid groupthink is to use devil's advocacy—presenting an opposing view to stir discussion and clarification, and dialectic—a method that ensures the team does not put a moral righteous spin on its decision making. The dialectic process involves debating. *Dialectic* is to debate two good ideas to determine the strengths and weaknesses of both before selecting one. Generally, when one person comes up with an idea, others will add to it or look at it from a different perspective. It is best to assign one or two members the task of asking the hard questions. To come up with the best solution, the group must look at many ideas. If the group is intercultural, you may have to ask people to give you their ideas. You also want to avoid letting one person dominate the discussions and to encourage many ideas and lots of feedback in discussions.

Work group time orientation is also influenced by the individual's view of flexibility, separation, and concurrency. *Flexibility* is the degree of rigidity placed on the use of time. It can range from the avoidance of scheduling, to having rigid meeting times, to being fluid where time is concerned. *Separation* is allowing or eliminating extraneous factors when working on a task. *Concurrency* is the number of tasks a person feels comfortable completing at the same time. While team participation may take up a large segment of a worker's time, other work assignments may require that the team member segregate team and individual work time. Ways to practice separation or inclusion include keeping your door closed or open; screening or taking calls, texts, and e-mails; and using nonverbal cues to indicate availability.

The team behaviors just discussed generally work well when everyone is from one culture and is in the same room together; however, virtual teams often do not have the luxury of either. Time elements, or chronemics, for virtual teams can have major consequences. Not only are people frequently in different time zones but how they perceive and use time may be different. Whether you are monochronic (can do one thing at a time) or polychronic (can do multiple tasks at the same time), in today's work world you have to be able to adjust to the other's time culture. Working globally is commonplace in today's organizations.

Currently, over 60 percent of professional employees participate in virtual teams (Kanawattanachai and Yoo 2007). It is possible for the members to be from only one national culture (such as the U.S. culture, which is actually made up of multiple cultures); however, that is not what is normal in today's work world. Virtual teams, by definition, are geographically dispersed, electronically dependent, have dynamic structural arrangements, and are often nationally diverse. Virtual teams must overcome the challenges that each of these elements represents in order to be innovative. Innovative organizations are adept at diversifying, adapting, and reinventing themselves to meet the changing global economy; and effective group interactions are critical to these processes. There is a great deal that virtual team members may not know about one another, including their situation, how they acquire knowledge, and their resources, so it is important for virtual team members to learn about one another before they can be an effective team. Many virtual teams find that not being in real time makes it difficult to keep a dynamic-innovative platform moving forward owing to time lags. Innovation tends to be better when teams do not have to rely only on electronic means of communication, though face-to-face opportunities may not be possible. Audio and video conferencing and social media tools can help to bridge the geographic divide. Because interactions are structured and recorded, many times virtual groups feel they are being micromanaged. When teams perceive a safer communication climate, more innovation takes place (Gibson and Gibbs 2006). Climate and culture will always influence the ethical practices of an organization and the types of moral problems managers will encounter.

Summary

The study of MC is a combination of management and communication theory. Because it is a relatively new discipline, testing continues both academically and in corporations. Theory testing and the scientific process support MC as being the main communication in the workplace; it overlaps with management, corporate communication, business communication, and organizational communication. Managers lead, plan, organize, and control the material, financial, informational, and human resources of a business by using MC.

The purpose of communicating in an organization is to get a message understood, see that the message accomplishes its purpose, and maintain favorable relationships with the people involved. Managers communicate information according to their position on the hierarchical level. The three levels of management include the strategic level, which is top management and deals with conceptual problems of the organization, the tactical level, which is middle management and controls more of the human elements of the organization, and the operational level, made up of frontline managers who generally are dealing with the technical skills of the organization.

MC is oriented more toward business management and communication theory than toward the skills of business communication. MC is the result of the merging of the types of professional communication in the workplace. Communication competency is the use by a manager of a combination of knowledge, skills, behaviors, and attitudes. Management is the art of getting things done using people in the right way, while satisfying their needs and the needs of the organization. Managers make decisions based on an understanding of the structure of the organization. One of the major problems today is an overabundance of information in the work world. Managers will need to sort through the information and be precise in the messages they send and receive.

Organizations can have formal communication policies or allow policies to develop ad hoc, or they may do both. The degree of formal or informal communication depends on how the firm is organized. The introduction of team-based management in the late 1970s moved firms from very formal communication to more informal communication. Team-based management relaxed the formal communication structure in favor of more informal lines of communication. Organizations learned that the quicker information could travel to where decisions were made or the actual work was being done, the more effective the organization became. The prevalence of virtual teams in today's innovative organizations has presented distinct challenges and opportunities for effective team communication and problem solving.

CHAPTER 2

The Managerial
Communication Process

Objectives

After reading this chapter, you will be able to:

1. describe the levels of managerial communication;
2. explain the main components of the communication process model;
3. discuss barriers to communication in the communication process;
4. identify ways to improve the communicative process.

Introduction

Managers have very different ways of communicating with coworkers, subordinates, and superiors. Effective managers can be abrupt, kind, or even forceful with others when needed. Managers communicate on different levels inside and outside the organizations, as well throughout the global economy. It is impossible to plan, organize, lead, or control business resources without effective communication skills.

Communication competency includes the ability to decipher and respond to what others are saying, and to understand why they communicate in the way they do, whether expressed directly or indirectly, and verbally or nonverbally. The communication process takes place on five levels: intrapersonal, interpersonal, group, organizational, and intercultural. These levels are frequently not mutually exclusive in a given communication situation.

Levels of Managerial Communication

Imagine you just scored two free tickets to your favorite basketball team on Monday. If you do not use the tickets, there is no refund available. Thus, your unused tickets will go to waste. What will you do? Deciding by yourself whether to attend the game, pass the tickets along to someone else, or let the tickets go to waste is an example of intrapersonal communication. Texting your best friend to determine his or her willingness to accompany you to the game is an example of interpersonal communication. Sending a text message to six of your close friends, telling them that the tickets are available, and that the first two to reply will receive the tickets is group communication. Offering your tickets to a business client who will be visiting from China on game day is an example of intercultural communication. In fact, if your first language is English and you practice a few sentences of Mandarin to use in offering the client the tickets, you are using several levels of communication. If your tone, quality, and pronunciation in Mandarin are exact, the gesture might payoff with your client in the future. Let us examine each level of communication in more detail.

Intrapersonal Communication

Intrapersonal communication is communicating within yourself. Intrapersonal communication involves the processes that occur inside an individual's brain. When you interpret ideas to clarify the meaning of what you see and hear, you are engaging in intrapersonal communication. Intrapersonal means that you ascribe meaning to the symbols and cues that exist in your environment. We are constantly engaging in intrapersonal communication with ourselves in our minds and thoughts.

Interpersonal Communication

Interpersonal communication requires interaction between you and another person. A dyad exists—two people communicating. During interpersonal communication you share a message with someone else. If both communicators share the same meaning, the message achieves its purpose and is understood. The intention and interpretation of a message must be correctly understood in order to be successful. Each person creates meaning in an exchange process, and they may or may not ascribe the same meaning to the message. Interpersonal communication elevates the message exchange and adds complexity; it also introduces the possibility that information can be misinterpreted or not be received at all.

Group Communication

Group communication involves three or more people in the process. Managers engage in this type of communication when they have meetings. Groups are generally small so that everyone can participate in discussions. Nonverbal and cultural issues can plague group communication. Consideration of the organizational climate is essential when there are international or host countries involved in the communication and decision making.

Generally groups learn to adapt, use structural intervention, and avoid the need for excessive managerial intervention, or they will part ways. Adaptation can be a problem. Adaptation happens when team members on both sides identify and acknowledge the differences they share and find ways to strategically work around them. Subdivision of the team's tasks happens with structural intervention, so that the tasks are separated according to discipline. With managerial intervention, the team can become overly dependent on the manager. When the members part ways, generally it is a loss for all sides. It is not easy to adjust to group situations, but with the correct attitude, strong solutions are possible.

Organizational Communication

An organization is a social group of people who have different strengths but common goals. To achieve these goals, they interact through the organization's communication processes and develop successful patterns and practices. Effective organizational communication requires knowledge of the structure. Many organizations, for instance, are virtual, multicultural, and multilingual. Technology is also changing how organizations communicate. To communicate effectively, you need to have knowledge about the channels through which the organization communicates. You must also be sensitive to the organization's leadership styles.

Intercultural Communication

Intercultural communication requires knowledge and understanding of culture. Managers who engage in effective intercultural communication must understand the norms and standards of the country, organizational norms, and the values and beliefs of the people within the culture. Intercultural communication also involves understanding of symbolic meanings that different cultures ascribe to nonverbal behaviors people exhibit in their social interactions.

Many challenges exist for international work teams. Team members from one cultural group may use direct communication, while others prefer indirect communication. U.S. citizens tend to be direct; however, Japanese are generally very indirect. Those from indirect cultures do not like to say no or make others lose face. Accents and fluency can be a problem, even if everyone is speaking English. Who does not have a story about calling a U.S. company's customer service phone number and speaking to someone in India, Pakistan, or Indonesia? Also, attitudes toward hierarchy and authority are different around the world. Mexicans view their boss very paternalistically; while in the United States, workers look at their boss as a businessperson. Conflicting norms for decision making can also cause problems. While U.S. business people want to make decisions very quickly, the Koreans often want to revisit and discuss items for longer periods of time before making decisions. This may mean that they revisit issues the Americans think have already been decided.

Cultural differences often result in a bias that one's own culture is superior to any other culture: *ethnocentrism*. Communicators can sometimes have stereotypes about each other. *Stereotypes* may include overgeneralizations about the other person's interpretation of time, personal space requirements, body language, and translation limitations. One learns about culture over time, and language transmits culture. Language controls thought processes; and therefore, the variations of thought processes between cultures. Some are deductive in their reasoning processes and others are inductive. Recognizing that people from other cultures may have different thought patterns is important when communicating and negotiating. Because we know our own culture very well, we do not have to think about it; however, when communicating with someone from another culture, we need to think about the similarities and differences that exist between us.

While the numerous cultures in the United States can cause communication challenges, the issue is now exacerbated even further by people who perceive themselves as members of an oppressed culture under constant attack by an oppressor culture. Oppression politics, also known as identity politics, has caused major rifts among the numerous cultures within the United States. These conflicts disrupt harmony and thwart goodwill among cultures separated by ethnic, racial, and gender differences.

Those who live within a minority culture might share an overriding set of customs that provide standards for behavior. If you unknowingly break a cultural rule, you could destroy a business relationship, see 50 percent of your advertisers flee, get sued, or be labeled racist, sexist, xenophobe, or homophobe. Your career can be destroyed by accusation alone, if the media puts you on trial in the court of public opinion for violating boundary limits of one of the subcultures existing within the American culture. Such snafus could be either verbal or nonverbal. *Nonverbals* include gestures, body language, facial expressions, dress, hairstyles, tattoos, and other outward signs that make verbals more or less believable. Some cultural norms that appear shocking to some may appear perfectly as normal, expected behaviors to others, as can be seen in the Window into Practical Reality 2.1.

Window into Practical Reality 2.1

Is Cultural Appropriation a Real Thing?

People commonly referred to online as "social justice warriors or SJWs" soldier the issues of their identity politics by direct confrontation with people from the oppressor class whom they perceive to have violated the boundary limits of their oppressed people's culture. When SJWs believe that a member of the oppressor class has taken something of value from the oppressed peoples' culture, they believe that *cultural appropriation* has occurred. SJWs tend to act in ways to reify their social construction of reality. They feel justified in confronting others, or attacking in some cases, irrespective of how shocking their behavior appears to objective third-party observers.

Cultural appropriation is perceived to be a real thing, which makes it hard for people to coexist peacefully in the larger American culture, especially when SJWs identify more as members of an oppressed culture (i.e., black and brown people as oppressed versus white people as oppressor) rather than all coexisting together in harmony as proud citizens of the United States of America. The ideology of political identity supersedes national pride because the politics seemingly become the identity of the person. Therefore, saying the pledge of allegiance, singing along with the national anthem, or saluting the American flag are taboo because these sacred words and actions belong to the oppressor class. Proselytes of identity politics have little interest in adhering to the unifying elements of the American culture. They perceive themselves as moral crusaders when they identify with a seemingly oppressed group (i.e., multimillionaire professional football athletes feel completely justified in taking a knee during the playing of the national anthem).

One distressing example of an SJW enforcing the boundary limits of cultural appropriation comes from an incident at San Francisco State University, which happened in 2016, where two people of color confronted a white student with accusations that he had appropriated the hair style of Egyptian or black culture. Bonita Tindle (a black female student) and her friend (a black male student) appeared to detain a white male student when they perceived the dreadlock hairstyle he was wearing was too close to dreadlocks often wore by people of African or Egyptian descent.

The white student asked, "You're saying that I can't have a hairstyle because of your culture? Why?"

Tindle responded: "Because it's my culture. Do you know what locks mean?"

The encounter became physical when the white male student attempted to leave the encounter but was blocked from leaving, grabbed by his arm, spun around, and pulled forward by Ms. Tindle so that she could continue her rebuke of the young man for his crime of cultural appropriation.

The 46-second YouTube video of the encounter published on March 28, 2016, by Nicholas Silvera went viral and sparked debate among many. It caught the attention of Mark Dice, a video blogger known for his sardonic ridicule of what he refers to as "liberals" or as people on the far left. During the final few seconds of the video, Ms. Tindle asked the camera man, "Why you filming this?!" The camera man replied, "For everyone's safety!"

Did Ms. Tindle have a right to detain and reprimand the white male student for his choice of hairstyle? What does this encounter tell us about the divergent world views in American culture? Why did Ms. Tindle see this as inappropriate rather than as an affirmation of her culture?

Source: www.youtube.com/watch?v=jDlQ4H0Kdg8.

Your managerial success is largely determined by your mastery of seven nonverbal elements (1) chronemics, (2) proxemics, (3) oculesics, (4) olfactics, (5) haptics, (6) facial expressions, and (7) chromatics.

How you view punctuality, the distance you stand from another person when in conversation, the clothes you wear, your jewelry, and even your word choice can become a barrier to effective managerial communication (MC). *Nonverbal barriers* are anything other than words that distract the recipient or lead to distortions that interfere with the reception of your intended message. Nonverbal differences happen across many dimensions of culture including language, gender, and generational divides. Basically, you have to learn about what you might encounter and not be afraid to ask questions when there is a nonverbal action that you do not understand. For example, in many Asian cultures personal silence in meetings is a signal that you need to call on individuals to get them to express their ideas. Culturally, nonverbals can have very different and often opposing meanings. As such it is best to avoid as many nonverbals as possible when communicating with someone from another culture, unless you are very comfortable in your knowledge of the culture.

Chronemics involves attitudes toward time, which vary widely across cultures. Whether a culture is monochronic or polychronic can be very important to the success of a business deal. People from *monochronic* cultures take deadlines and meeting commitments seriously; they are punctual. People in *polychronic* cultures are not as punctual and do not take deadlines as seriously. Cultural norms shape perceptions of the importance of time, which differs between monochronic and polychronic cultures as seen in Figure 2.1. Some countries with monochronic cultures are the United States, England, Switzerland, and Germany. Some areas of the world with polychronic cultures are Latin America, Southern Europe, and the Middle East.

Differences in time systems	
Monochronic	**Polychronic**
Does one thing at a time	Does many things at once
Concentrates on the task	Are highly distractible and subject to interruptions
Takes time commitments seriously and value promptness	Considers time commitments more casually; promptness based on the relationship
Are committed to the task	Are committed to people
Shows respect for private property; rarely borrows or lends	Borrows and lends things often
Are accustomed to short-term relationships	Tend to build lifetime relationships

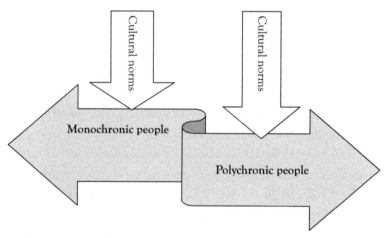

Figure 2.1 Time system differences between monochronic and polychronic cultures

Source: Chaney and Martin (2014, p. 118).

Differences in the concept of time may cause problems when trying to schedule online meetings, as someone from a monochronic culture will typically be online early or on time, while those from polychronic cultures may be engaged in something else that they feel is important and not join the online discussion on time. These cultural norms are neither correct nor wrong; they are merely noncongruent for team participants.

Proxemics, or the use of space, is another area of cultural difference. You might see differences in meeting room seating arrangements depending upon the proxemics of a culture. People in the United States have an intimate zone of less than 18 in for people they know very well, a casual-personal zone is 18 in to 4 ft, a social zone of 4 to 12 ft used with people with whom they work closely, and a public distance of over 12 ft for those they do not know (Hall, 1966). Cultural standards create different proxemics—some engage in hugging and kisses on the cheek or air kisses. In the United States a private office is considered a status symbol, whereas in Japan there are only a few, and even those are not used a great deal of the time. In France, the boss sits in the middle of the work area, with subordinates in offices around him or her.

Oculesics, or eye contact, is important because some cultures show respect by looking away, while others by almost staring, with many degrees of difference in between. Unfortunately, unbroken staring can be misinterpreted as hostility, aggressiveness, or intrusiveness when the intended meaning was just to appear interested. Minimal eye contact may be misinterpreted as lack of interest, understanding, dishonesty, fear, or shyness when the intended meaning was to show respect or to avoid appearing intrusive. In some cultures, one shows respect to women by not looking them in the eye; even though a man would normally have direct eye contact with another male.

Olfactics, or smell, can significantly affect communications. Smell impresses itself very strongly on our memories and remains long after the person has gone. Hygiene, perfumes, and what one eats are the main sources of personal smell. In business situations, it is important to bath regularly, use breath fresheners, refrain from perfumes, and have an understanding that what you eat or drink is secreted through your skin which others can smell.

Haptics, or touch, is interpreted very differently around the world. Knowing the cultural norms and standards for how and where one may touch and whom one may touch is important. In many parts of the world, men greet each other with a hug of varying degrees of intimacy rather than a handshake or a bow. In some countries, touching the top of the head is inappropriate. While a slap on the back in the United States means that you have done a good job, in Japan it has the opposite meaning. It is important to consider and understand what the correct etiquette for touching is in the different cultures with whom you may come in contact. Senior clerics criticized President Mahmoud Ahmadinejad of Iran for hugging the mother of the deceased Venezuelan President Hugo Chavez at his funeral (Akbar 2013). Physical contact, considered a sin when touching an unrelated woman in the Islamic religion, is seen as empathetic in Venezuela where hugging is common. Cultures exist where it is not appropriate for a woman and man to even shake hands in public if nor related.

Facial expressions may not always be what they appear. For instance, laughing when embarrassed is not unusual for Asians. The degree of animation has a deep cultural basis, as do gestures and the amount of gesturing that goes on during a conversation. Until you know how someone from another culture understands a gesture, you should refrain from using it or explaining it.

Chromatics, or the use and interpretation of color, can also be important. For example, black is the color of mourning for many Europeans and Americans, while white is normally worn for funerals in Japan, and red has funeral connotations in African countries. Purple is associated with royalty in many countries, but with death in some Latin American countries. Colors are particularly important when exporting products for sale in other countries and in selecting gifts for business associates.

The Managerial Communication Model

All the levels of MC impact the MC process model. Figure 2.2 illustrates nine components of this model. The model depicts two layers: the macroenvironment and microenvironment. The macroenvironment has an indirect influence on the communication and includes (1) organizational culture and (2) situational context. The microenvironment has a direct influence on the communication and includes (3) information source, (4) encoding, (5) message over channel, (6) decoding, (7) destination, (8) barriers, and (9) feedback.

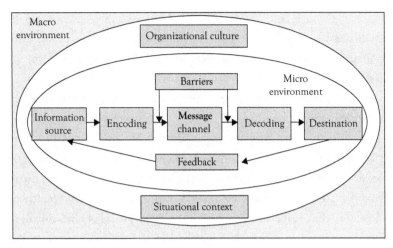

Figure 2.2 Model of managerial communication

The first process model evolved from engineering practices from the past. Claude E. Shannon, an engineer for the Bell Telephone Company, introduced one of the most influential early models of the communication process to study issues of interdepartmental workflow (Weaver 1949). Later Shannon and Weaver (1949) added a corrective element to the model called feedback. This feature makes this model an interpersonal process. The model has been changed over the years to reflect current research and practice.

The MC model has been very helpful in advancing communication theories in organizational, corporate, business, and managerial communication.

Organizational Culture

Culture consists of shared values, symbols, meanings, practices, customs and traditions, history, tacit understandings, habits, norms, expectations, common meanings, rites, and shared assumptions. Just as countries and regions of the world have their own cultures, so does each organization. *Organizational culture* includes the behaviors developed through rules, regulations, and procedures that promote the attainment of the goal. People within an organization share organizational culture just as ethnic groups share ethnic culture. Organizational culture determines how to do things through common agreement. The way workers interact socially at work assists in defining organizational culture. Communication helps to disseminate cultural expectations and bind the organizational culture together.

Coordinating and directing employees involves trade-offs. The difficult part for the management is to get all the workers in an organization to view the direction or goals of the firm in the same way. This is why it is not unusual for there to be subcultures within an organization. If the subcultures get prominent, effective communication is jeopardized. If subcultures diverge from the mission of the firm, they can actually be harmful to the organization. Generally, however, goals help individuals to learn their position within the organization and the firm's expectations. Managers must realize, however, that workers' perceptions of information, their thought patterns, and their values may be very different from the managers' perceptions. When an individual's values match those of the organization, job satisfaction increases.

Managers of international organizations must consider the cultural differences among the countries that are working together. This includes understanding differences in the laws, culture, and working climate of the countries involved. When group norms are different, it is not always easy for people to adapt to one another. However, if the groups can be taught to recognize and appreciate these differences, it is easier for them to understand and work together. Language also plays a major role in developing our mindset and how we think. When someone is speaking a second language, they are often in the mindset of their first language. Therefore, people may not interpret messages in the way they were intended by the sender. In fact, there may not at times be equivalent words to express some thoughts or ideas between the two languages.

In order to manage an organizational culture, top management must have a strategic plan, develop cultural leaders, share the culture by communicating effectively with staff, measure performance, communicate culture to employees, and motivate them. Doing this requires trade-offs between the members of the organization at all levels. In order to accomplish the mission of the organization, some people will typically strive to gain power, while expecting others to surrender some of their flexibility and independence. When working within the corporate culture, you will need to remember that you are working with social elements that may or may not seem rational.

Continuing dialog will help all of us understand each other, but mistakes will happen. The larger the organization, the more opportunities there are for miscommunications due to cultural differences. Along with continuing dialog, we must also consider the particular situation in which the communication is happening.

Situational Context

The situational context is another component of the macroenvironment of the MC process. Is the situation critical, meaning is it dangerous or imminent, or does it involve planning for the future? The situational context will often determine to whom the communication is made and what channel is chosen to achieve the communication. Situational factors include gender, age, cultural differences, as well as whether the relationship is with a subordinate, peer, or superior.

We will now continue our discussion with the seven components of the microenvironment involved in the MC process.

Information Source

An *information source* is the person from whom the communication originates. When you call on a customer or an employee and give them a message, you are the information source. The *message* is the information you want the receiver to act upon. In creating a message, you encode it.

Encoding

When you create meaning which will be sent to a targeted recipient, you are *encoding* the message. When doing this, you must consider many things about the person or persons receiving the message. The more you know about your audience, the easier it is to communicate with them because you have an idea of how they will respond to what you say. Audience characteristics include age, economic level, educational background, and culture.

Channel

A *channel* is the medium through which the message travels. E-mail, memorandum, letter, text, telephone, social media, fax, face-to-face, meeting, and company newspaper are examples of channels. *Channel selection* can be determined by how soon the recipients need the information, confidentiality of the information, the hierarchical relationship of the communicators, the location, gender, culture, and level of education of the recipient.

Decoding

The person receiving the communication has to decode the message just as the information source encoded it. However, we all have different screens through which we filter messages. When you decode, you interpret and translate the message you have received according to your mindset. The more alike we are, the more likely our message will be understood as it was intended to be. The more different we are, the more room there is for mistakes in decoding, both in interpreting and in translating the message incorrectly.

Destination

The person or people receiving and interpreting the message are the *destination.* The recipient can be a person or a group receiving a message that you send. The recipient, or destination, of a message can be intended or unintended. No matter how hard you work to make it perfect, there will be some distortion in the message.

Barriers

Barriers are a given in any form of communication. *Barriers* are items that interfere with the message. Barriers include physical or psychological problems, language, gender issues, education-level issues, generational issues, and nonverbal differences.

Physical and *psychological* barriers can distort the message. Physical and psychological barriers may include disabilities, health problems, parental issues, elder-care issues, money problems, or mental issues. Any of these barriers can impact a person's work. How a manager handles the physical and psychological problems of subordinates is important. The ability to handle subordinates' issues is influenced by the manager's knowledge of the situation and the personalities of those involved. Given that people are going to experience some difficulties during their lives, it is generally better for the manager to exhibit compassion and try to find a solution to problems rather than to put more pressure on employees for things beyond their control.

Language barriers happen even if both sides speak the same language. There are dozens of different dialects of English spoken as a first language across the world. Many others are taught variations of those dialects of English because English is the number one language used in business around the world. However, just because two people are speaking English, it does not mean that they understand each other. The spelling, definition, and pronunciation of words can all be different. English is not the only language in which this happens, so if you learn another language you must realize that there are variations in the languages used throughout the world. Translation from one language to another adds additional challenges, as it is not always possible to translate idiomatic expressions from one language to another.

Gender barriers arise even among those within the same culture. Problems are magnified by the fact that expectations for behavior and interaction vary widely with gender. The gender barriers range from the recognition of complete equality between the genders to very strict rules that separate the genders. In China and Japan, for instance, women speak in a different tone than men when expressing the same point of view. In orthodox Islamic areas of the world, girls and boys do not attend school together, which means that girls do not have the same resources available or subjects to study as the boys have. In many cases, men and women are not allowed to work together in Islamic countries. Therefore, there are many communication strategies to be considered when communicating with an individual who is different both culturally and in gender.

Research has shown that the gender of the participants, the team's overall gender composition, and the gender orientation of the task influences the feedback-seeking behavior among team members (Miller and Karakowsky 2005). Because they are more concerned about interpersonal relationships and generally more compassionate, women are more open to feedback than men (London, Larsen, and Thisted 1999). The type of position and whether it is a traditional or nontraditional one has a direct effect on the method women use to obtain feedback (Holder 1996). The requirements of the task may emphasize gender-differentiated skills that increase gender differences within the group. Studies have shown that men seek feedback more on male-oriented tasks within a male group, and females are less likely to seek feedback in a female group performing a male-oriented task. Women in mainly male groups and masculine-oriented tasks are more likely to seek feedback than are women in male groups with female-oriented tasks. When expertise is clearly present in both genders, both groups seek feedback; however, men tend to not seek feedback in situations that are not involved with masculine-oriented tasks. As more women enter the workforce, fewer and fewer positions are considered to be female- or male-specific jobs.

The *educational levels* between and among people can also be a communication barrier. You want to control your vocabulary and sentence structure when communicating with people below or above you both inside and outside the organization. The more you know about the people you are communicating with, the better you can choose words and sentence structure that will help them decode your messages correctly. A manager in a manufacturing plant where the workers typically have only a high school education would want to communicate at approximately an eighth-grade school level rather than at a college level. Most newspapers are written at a sixth- to eighth-grade school level. Did you know that you can check the grade level of your written messages while using Microsoft Word?

Generational differences are a large barrier to communication in organizations. As Table 2.1 illustrates, there are five generations of communicators in the workplace who impact the effectiveness of your success in the MC process. While historians and sociologists differ somewhat on the exact years that differentiate the generations, there is general agreement on the characteristics of each group. If you were born between 1925 and 1945, you are a traditionalist. If you were born between 1946 and 1965, you are a Boomer. If you were born between 1966 and 1979, you are a Gen Xer. If you were born between 1980 and 1999, you are a millennial.

Table 2.1 World views and communication efficacy between and among the four generations

World views	Traditionalists	Boomers	Gen Xers	Millennials	Gen Zers
Birth periods	1925 through 1945	1946 through 1965	1966 through 1979	1980 through 1999	2000 through present
View of work	Work is expected; hard work is good in itself	Work goal is to meet or surpass one's own expectations of success	Work is considered self-fulfillment	Work is synonymous with continuous learning and change	Prone to shifting attitudes about work and will quit the organization abruptly in conflict situations
View of authority	Respectful	Love–hate	Unimpressed	Polite	Cautious
View of change	Get it over with	Create it	Make it work for you	Recognize it as inevitable and increasing	Embrace rapid change
View of decision making	Hierarchy	Consensus	Competence	Team cooperation	Shared online experiences
View of feedback	No news is good news	Yearly documented feedback	Lots of positive feedback	Instantaneous feedback	Social media drama/trends (i.e., online bullying, #metoo, #notmypresident) will influence acceptance
Communicating with	Do not expect them to share their thoughts immediately; Focus on words rather than body language or inferences use face-to-face or written communication; Do not waste their time	Use body language when communicating with the "Show Me" generation; Speak in an open, direct style; but avoid controlling language; Answer questions thoroughly and expect to be pressed for details; Present options to demonstrate flexibility in your thinking	Use e-mail as a primary channel; Talk in short sound bits to keep their attention; Ask for their feedback and provide them with input; Share information with them on a regular basis and strive to keep them in the loop; Use an informal communication style	Use action words and challenge them at every opportunity; Avoid talking down to them; Use texts and Facebook IMs over e-mail and e-mail over face-to-face communication; Seek feedback constantly and provide them with feedback; Use humor and create fun learning environments; Do not take yourself too seriously as they will not; Encourage them to take risks to explore new ways of learning	Use social media, in addition to more traditional means, to communicate and share information. Provide opportunities for them to apply the use of emergent technologies that are appropriate to work processes. Clarify facts, as they are often quick to believe unverified online information and can be prone to spread and propagate false information Use of Snapchat, Instagram, Twitter and Facebook Messenger is the very best way to keep Gen Zers informed and to stay informed about them

Sources: Snyder, 2010; Desai and Lele 2017.

If you were born between 2000 and the present, you are a Gen Zer. Effective managers recognize generational issues and communication preferences that differentiate Traditionalists, Boomers, Gen Xers, Millennials, and Gen Zers.

Intergenerational issues are the communication gaps that exist because of age and behavior patterns among various groups of individuals. Each group has habits that are broadly defined by their life experiences. Boomers are more likely to use e-mail and voice messaging rather than texting or sending tweets, which Millennials routinely do. Traditionalists might not even use computers on a daily basis. Imagine the barrier this habit alone would create if a millennial is attempting to tweet a Traditionalist who probably does not even have a Twitter account.

The oldest generation cohort likely to be in the workplace are *Traditionalists*, born between 1925 and 1945. They are considered to be loyal, highly dedicated, and risk-averse employees (Jenkins 2008). They place a high emphasis on interpersonal communication, obey the rules, value a top–down management style, and rarely question authority (Kyles 2005). Therefore, Traditionalists will expect face-to-face communication with their boss, will probably not carry a smartphone, and may only be involved with e-mail and Facebook because of their grandchildren.

Baby Boomers were born between 1946 and 1965. Boomers tend to be workaholics. Most have had to learn technology in the workplace but still appreciate face-to-face conversations. They use smartphone, e-mail, and text messaging, and many also use social media.

Gen Xers were born between 1966 and 1979 and represent the smallest generational cohort in numbers. Many were born into homes with two working parents and are considered the latchkey generation. They are self-reliant and have carried this characteristic into the workplace (Macon and Artley 2009). Unlike their Boomer parents, Xers place more emphasis on a work–life balance, often choosing personal life over work. Xers are pragmatic, adaptable, entrepreneurial, skeptical, and distrustful of authority (Arnsparger 2008).

Millennials were born between 1980 and 1999. Technology, September 11, 2001, the Columbine School shooting, and the increasing ease of obtaining information via the Internet have helped to shape this generation. Some call them digital natives because they do not remember a time without technology. Millennials like structure, open communication, and direct access to senior management (Hershatter and Epstein 2010).

Gen Zers were born between 2000 and the present and represent the generation of young people who never knew the world without the Internet. Two in five Gen Zers are born to unmarried mothers. U.S. statistics from 2016 indicated that proportion to be 69.8 percent among blacks, 52.6 percent among Hispanics, and 28.5 percent among whites (Martin et al. 2018). As a result, many Gen Zers come from homes where a female is the head of household, and many do not have a connection with their biological fathers. Gen Zers are adept at social media and are used to having information speedily at their fingertips. This technology savvy generation share and retain constant communication via digital media (Desai and Lele 2017). Gen Zers' identities can be directly connected to an online image of themselves; and they also can be influenced by ideological beliefs that they derived from their social network connections, not necessarily germane to a healthy connection with others. Table 2.1 gives some ideas on the views and ways to communicate effectively among the five generations.

When communicating the corporate strategy, organizations expect everyone in the firm to share a common view of where the organization is going. However, if all levels of communication are not addressed, this may not be possible. Given the generational differences that exist in most work environments, it is important for a manager to employ various strategies including intergenerational education, succession planning, mentoring, and technology education. Managers who take the time to develop a multigenerational communication strategy generally experience greater cohesion, trust, innovation, and collaboration across generations.

The downward flow of communication should be offered in multiple formats to ensure that everyone receives information in a timely manner. While Traditionalists and Boomers may prefer face-to-face verbal exchanges, Gen Xers, Millennials, and Gen Zers may prefer texting, e-mail, or corporate broadcasts. As the younger generations replace Traditionalists and Boomers, mentoring between the generations becomes very important. This means that mentors need to be educated about how to communicate successfully with the Gen Xers, Millennials, and Gen Zers; and mentees need to understand when face-to-face and verbal communication is preferable to the technology-assisted channels. Corporate education is a must for all generations as can be seen in Window into Practical Reality 2.2.

Window into Practical Reality 2.2

Generational Difference in Information Sharing and Retrieval

Millennials may use libraries, but only through the Internet—many have never set foot in a library building. While Traditionalists and Boomers will generally opt for the newspaper for business news, Gen Xers and Millennials will want to read the news as it happens on their electronic devices. Gen Zers force the issues by being directly involved in helping to shape news, not merely consuming it. They are more prone to engage in physical reactions to what they experience online as vital to themselves. Rather than disengaging from social networks that offend the user, they can take extreme actions. Some younger Gen Zers have gone so far as to attempt or actually commit irreversible actions (i.e., suicide because of cyberbullying). Unlike other generations, Gen Zers are passionately connected to their online worlds via Facebook Messenger and Twitter. Business Insider's Maya Kosoff (2016) reports that "80% of teenagers they surveyed said they used Facebook Messenger as a primary or secondary form of communicating with friends." A factor for all generations to consider is whether maintaining a history of the communication is required or advisable; with texting you do not have a way to save the communication for historical purposes, but you do with e-mail and other written forms of communication.

Generational issues present many problems for management including conflicts in the workplace that can result in reduced profitability, hiring challenges, increased turnover, and a decrease in morale between the generations (Macon and Artley 2009).

Managers with a multigenerational staff need to be aware of the different preferred modes of communication. The Millennials and Gen Zers are early adopters of new technology using texting first, phone second, e-mail third, and other mediums after that. While Generation Xers are computer savvy, they are not attached to their computers and handhelds in the way Millennials are. Boomers learned their computer knowledge on their own, on the job, and have less formal training in technology than their younger counterparts. Traditionalists have primarily learned enough about technology to communicate with their grandchildren. The ability to use computer-mediated communication (CMC) is one of the main differences between the generations. One of the main problems with CMC is that while it is quick, it is basically devoid of nonverbal communication. Some companies have instituted non-CMC days because people were using CMC to communicate with those sitting next to them. On technology-free days, people must get up and go see the person they need to communicate with if they are in the same building. Challenges can emerge when elitist attitudes develop among generational workers. Social Identity Theory recognizes that members of the various groups may see themselves as superior to other groups because of either their long-term knowledge of the company or their CMC knowledge.

Corporation memory is changing. Knowledge transfer methods are changing. Cross-generational teams offer the best avenue for moving organizations forward, though challenges exist in making them work effectively. Gen Xers, Millennials, and Gen Zers are more open to the informal nature of teamwork, whereas the Traditionalist and Boomers accustomed to working alone early in their careers have had to learn to work on teams. Millennials and Gen Zers also tend to get bored very easily which can cause increased turnover. As younger generational groups join the workforce, challenges for effective communication across generational divides will continue.

While there are many differences, there are also similarities between the generations. Those of all generations want to feel valued, empowered, and engaged at work. While the Gen Xers, Millennials, and Gen Zers are more vocal about flexibility, Boomers and Traditionalists also want some flexibility.

Feedback

When the destination receives your message and encodes a response, the process of *feedback* happens. While the destination may or may not give the feedback that is expected, the quality of the feedback will be determined by the level of barriers. If barriers are small, the destination will send correct or favorable feedback to the source. If barriers are large, the destination will send incorrect or unfavorable feedback. If a distorted message reaches the destination, the destination might not interpret the message properly and as such there will be no feedback or the feedback may not be applicable. However, you might construe no feedback at all an indication that the message was not received—or, if you are a bit paranoid, you might construe your message as being ignored. Never assume your destination has ignored your message. For e-mail and voice messages, give the recipient 24 hours to respond, and for old-fashioned USPS "snail" mail, give the recipient a week to respond. If possible, respond in kind in terms of the message channel. Return a call with a call, a text with a text, and e-mail with an e-mail. This assures that your channel selection will be correct, especially when the communication is with someone outside of your generational population.

Improving the Communicative Process

There are three main reasons why messages can fail in the communication process (1) framing effects, (2) illusion of control, and (3) discounting the future.

Framing effects occur when the decision is influenced by the way the problem or issue is phrased, thus helping or hurting any chance of selecting the preferred alternative. Choices can be presented in a way that highlights the positive or negative aspects of the same decision, leading to changes in their relative attractiveness. Negative framing predisposes the recipient to a negative opinion of the issue.

Illusion of control refers to scenarios in which managers believe they can control the outcome or influence events even though they may not have control. When managers argue that they can control or predict all the variables, they are usually delusional. Experienced managers might know they have succeeded in the past, but they also should be aware that past success is no guarantee of a future outcome. Believing an outcome is guaranteed and selling this notion to others is illusion of control. The illusion of control is exhibited when a manager argues, vehemently, that the competition "could never . . ." or "I doubt very seriously that . . .," when there is no evidence other than emotional hunches.

Discounting the future occurs when managers use communication tactics that lead to a preference for short-term benefits at the expense of longer-term cost and benefits. Corporate leaders can fall victim to the pressures of making money for shareholders while distributing earning to owners. Nevertheless, pressure to impress can create a dangerous rhetoric that leads managers to value short-term profits over long-term competitive advantages for their business.

Use the MC model to dissect your own approach to business communication and scrutinize positive and negative examples of the communication of others. Learning to decipher and understand what others are saying and perhaps why they communicate the way they do, whether they say it directly or indirectly, can be important to you personally and to your company. The communication process model reflects the theories that underlie communication and breaks the process into elements that helps managers navigate the challenging communication process.

Summary

There are five levels of MC: intrapersonal, interpersonal, group, organizational, and intercultural. Intrapersonal communication involves the processes that occur inside an individual's thoughts. Interpersonal communication involves another person with whom you interact. To manage effectively, recognize generational issues and communication preferences that differentiate Traditionalists, Boomers, Gen Xers, Millennials, and Gen Zers. Group communication involves three or more persons. Organizational communication requires knowledge of structural expectations. Intercultural communication requires knowledge of other cultures.

The nine components of the MC process model depict two layers: the macroenvironment including organizational culture and situational context; and the microenvironment including information source, encoding, message over channel, decoding, destination, barriers, and feedback. Communication barriers include physical or psychological issues, language barriers, gender issues, education-level issues, and generational issues.

CHAPTER 3

Power, Climate, and Culture

Objectives

After reading this chapter, you will be able to:

1. explain communication context;
2. explain the power of leaders;
3. explain organizational communication climate;
4. discuss established levels of organizational culture;
5. differentiate formal from informal communication networks.

Introduction

Context is the physical, social, and psychological environment where the communication interaction takes place. Imagine a 45-year-old manager paying a compliment to a 22-year-old administrative assistant, who has just been hired, on her wardrobe. He tells her, "You look very professional today and ideal for our company." Much to the manager's chagrin, the administrative assistant asks, in a rather scornful tone, "What are you looking at?" She is loud enough for others passing by to hear. The manager, feeling confused and embarrassed, immediately apologizes and tells the young woman, "I am looking at nothing more than your wardrobe," he continues, "Have a good day, Ms. Jones." In this hypothetical example, the physical environment is the hallway. The social environment is the organization's culture and climate, where the manager is comfortable enough to pay a compliment to a young woman he barely knows without fear of accusation. Because the young woman was new to the company, she did not understand that she was receiving a compliment.

Communication Context

Understanding culture is essential to effective communication. Based on how an organization and its leaders view culture, behaviors can vary. Table 3.1 contains some well-established definitions of culture and corporate culture.

Table 3.1 Established definitions of culture and corporate culture

Deal and Kennedy (1982, p. 4)	Schein (1992, p. 12)	Sherriton and Stern (1997, p. 26)
. . . *culture* is "the integrated pattern of human behavior that includes thought, speech, action, and artifacts and depends on man's capacity for learning and transmitting knowledge to succeeding generations" or informally *corporate culture* is "the way we do things around here."	. . . *culture* is "a pattern of shared basic assumptions that the group learned as it solved its problems of external adaptation and internal integration, that has worked well enough to be considered valid; and therefore, to be taught to new members as the correct way to perceive, think, and feel in relation to those problems."	. . . *corporate culture* is [defined] more prescriptively as "the environment or personality of the organization, with all its multifaceted dimensions."

In the earlier example, the psychological environment exists individually, inside the minds of the manager and the administrative assistant. It is possible that the young woman harbors remnants of bad experiences. It is possible that she previously worked in an organization where sexual harassment existed in a climate of tolerance for such behavior. It is also possible the manager had just harassed the administrative assistant. Incidents of one individual harassing another under the veil of good intentions are not uncommon in business. Complimenting a woman's wardrobe while looking at her chest the whole time could be the reason for a young woman to react to a compliment with a scornful rebuke.

In this chapter, we will consider the power of leaders, organizational communication climate (OCC), and culture. First, as a manager you will need to understand the dynamics of the power that different types of leaders have within the communication context. Second, you will need to understand the climate of the organization in which you work. Third, you need to be able to navigate the levels of organizational culture and understand that culture is both visible and invisible.

The discussion begins with brief definitions of leadership and leaders. We will then explore the five powers of leaders in context.

Power of Leaders

Leadership is a process to provide forward movement for the organization—visions for the future. *Managerial leadership* is a process used to influence employees to reach the common goals of the corporation. Reaching the firm's goals is easier when managers lead and strive to achieve common goals for the good of all. An organization must have both managers and leaders to succeed, though they are not always one and the same. Leaders need to be able to listen and hear in order to influence employees. They need to be informed and ask others' opinions about current situations and new ideas. Leaders influence others to reach common goals—mostly through their communication efforts. The five bases of influence that give leaders power are (1) referent power, (2) expert power, (3) legitimate power, (4) reward power, and (5) coercive power.

Referent Power

Referent power is based on the individual's personality. Power can be used for bad or good reasons, and some immoral communicators have led people to terrible ends by abusing their referent power. This was the case with Jim Jones in 1978. A preacher with incredible influence over his congregation, he convinced his followers that the end of days was happening. More than 900 of his followers, either willingly or under duress, drank a punch laced with the highly lethal poison cyanide. That tragedy is now infamously known as the Jonestown Massacre. On the positive side, Warren Buffet can merely mention a stock as a personal like and people will flock to buy that stock. Oprah Winfrey can talk favorably about a book she has read, and overnight that book becomes a best seller. Many others have gained power based on their personal charisma or level of knowledge in a field or industry.

The Window into Practical Reality 3.1 exemplifies just how significant referent power and an attractive personality can be in the political arena.

Window into Practical Reality 3.1

The Unlikely Election of President Donald Trump—A Near Perfect Example of Referent Power and Rhetorical Skills

People in all walks of life and from every social class the world over, and especially those with the power over the media, predicted that Trump would never be president of the United States. Ironically, to their chagrin, the voting public made Donald John Trump president. He took the oath of office on January 20, 2017, with his hand on his family Bible and the Abraham Lincoln Bible, and became the 45th president of the United States of America.

There is nothing more interesting for people who study mass media and public discourse than to look at what occurred in the 2016 U.S. presidential election. The fact that Trump could defeat 16 established Republican candidates in the primaries and defeat a Democrat candidate, who seemed to have the mainstream media (MSM) clearly on her side, with his use of rhetoric and an appeal to nationalism has many scratching their heads in disbelief.

The verbal attacks on President Trump started long before his announcement that he would be running for president. In fact, it was the ridicule directed at him which seemed to transform his speaking style. His opponents introduced the very weapon that Trump used to defeat them. Because the MSM chose to air language that was historically viewed as vulgar and trite against Trump, they inadvertently set the rules for political discourse in the modern era. The media made ridicule and impoliteness fair game in airing grievances in the public arena. In other words, it seems President Trump's tactics emerged from a 2011 White House correspondents' dinner.

The comedic attacks on his intellectual abilities and character gave him tacit approval to use similar language against his opponents throughout the campaign for his presidency, including his daily Twitter posts. In 2011, the general consensus was that Donald Trump would never be president of the United States; it was said with certainty by many. At a White House correspondents' dinner, April 30, 2011, the comedian Seth Meyers and President Barack Obama cracked jokes about a potential Trump election; they, in a sense, used playground rules to triple-dog-dare him to run by depicting the billionaire business man as a simpleton or a fool.

Seth Meyers joked, "Donald Trump has been saying that he will run for president as a Republican, which is surprising since I just assumed he'd be running as a joke." The audience burst into roaring laughter. The billionaire Trump never cracked a smile. Meyers continued, "Donald Trump often appears on Fox, which is ironic because a fox often appears on Donald Trump's Head" (Fusion07mp4, YouTube 2011). The blistering attacks continued for several minutes, personal and vitriolic. President Barack Obama declared on a number of occasions, almost in a panic of disbelief nearing the end of the 2016 elections that "Donald Trump will never be president." Many on both the left (Democrat) and the right (Republican) of the political spectrum, despite their intense efforts, still do not understand why Trump is now president of the United States.

.With so much energized effort to prevent the Trump presidency, why did it happen?

President Trump's *referent power* comes from his natural ability to understand humor, and people are attracted to his personality because of his sense of humor. People should never crack jokes on people who are funnier than themselves. In a sense, the jokes against President Trump backfired because his ability to use humor strategically, his precise use of words, and his personality, combined with his business savvy, served as a cocktail of defeat for his much less able rhetorical rivals. Candidate Trump was able to infuse into his presidential campaign the *fallacy of name calling, ad hominin* insults on the person as campaign strategy, pilot tested in real time at his rallies. The ad hominin attacks did not consider the ideas of the opponents, but were purely *mockery* as a means to "misbrand" his political rivals, putting them off balance and on the defensive.

Candidate Trump's rivals were now playing in an arena that was foreign to them; they had little chance of redirecting the public's view back to their preferred brand (public image) once candidate Trump had tarnished their brand with one of his famous fallacies. For example, "Little Marco" for Marco Rubio, "Lying Ted" for Texas senator Ted Cruz, and "Low energy Jeb" for former Florida governor Jeb Bush. The blitzkrieg continued, with "Crooked Hilary." Rarely were any of the political rivals, Republican or Democrat, able to repair their damaged brands. When Rubio tried and failed, by referring to candidate Trump's hands as "small," this hurt his image even further and compounded his branding problems, especially in his home state of Florida. Carly Fiorina, former HP CEO, emotionally responded to Trump's barb directed at her when declaring that people should "look at her face, have you seen that face?" Her response of "every woman in America knows what Donald Trump meant," was both too tame and possibly alienated her male voting base. Feeble attempts to redress candidate Trump's rhetoric seemed to only worsen the branding issues for his political rivals. Their comebacks appeared boring and mundane.

Trump's misbranding efforts simply were funnier than his opponents' ineffective comebacks. Trump had the personality that attracted people to his message of nationalism, all while making the establishment politicians look more like what they had depicted him to be in 2011.

Source: www.youtube.com/watch?v=iWuv2txl_5M.

Expert Power

Expert power is based on competence. Expert power does not necessarily need to be explained; people just seem to know once a person with this type of power speaks. Many examples of this can be found in literature and in real life. The fictional character Sherlock Holmes had immense expert power. His reputation preceded him, because he had established a record of solving nearly impossible cases using inductive and deductive reasoning. In real life, few people would question the contributions to physics made by Albert Einstein $(E = MC^2)$; to literature made by Edgar Allen Poe (critical analysis of literature and the murder mystery); or to mathematics made by Rene Descartes (the father of analytic geometry and the Cartesian coordinate system). People with expert power are given respect through the deference of others. A person like Warren Buffet has both referent and expert power. Some leaders, however, acquire power by attaining position or status within an organization.

Legitimate Power

Legitimate power is based on the position or status earned or inherited. Some leaders have power because they earned it by climbing the corporate ladder, paying the price of hard work and sacrifice. Others might be born into a family that owns or has controlling shares of a business, and thus inherit a CEO position. In family owned businesses, succession planning typically names heirs to positions of power. In some cases, the person might not be the best suited for the position, yet could still be in control. Most organizations will have measures in place to ensure that only those who are competent are promoted within the structural hierarchy.

Reward Power

Reward power is based on the granting of positive stimuli to employees who work hard. A reward is a stimulus (positive reinforcement, tangible or intangible—verbal praise, a bonus, a certificate, flextime schedule, and more) used to reinforce a desired behavior exhibited by a subordinate. Rewards are used to keep behaviors consistent within the context of organized work routines. Leaders have power when they control things that others' want and for which they are willing to behave in a desired way in order to receive the reward. Psychologists refer to this behavior as conditioning. The use of rewards to modify subordinates' behaviors gives leaders extraordinary power of control.

Coercive Power

Coercive power is based on penalizing or punishing an employee. A punishment is a consequence imposed on an individual because he or she has engaged in an undesired behavior. Leaders sometimes supervise subordinates who will not respond to rewards. Personal and family problems, drug abuse, apathy, or feelings of inequity can result in nonresponse to a system of rewards. Some managers will use punishment to influence behaviors that they want subordinates to change. If a manager feels that a subordinate is unproductive or not supportive of the common goals, the manager may use coercive powers to get the person to either change or leave. "Two brains are better than one" is a cliché that is more often correct than incorrect, and this is why leaders often forge dyadic relationships with some employees. Leader–member exchange affords leaders power that can be very fruitful.

Climate

Organization communication climate is what you feel, hear, and sense when you watch employees interact. OCC includes degree of openness, trust, confidence, participation in decision making, and acceptance that exist in the work environment. Central to this humanistic approach to management is that subordinates participate in decision making. In an open and supportive climate, superiors and subordinates talk to each other, rather than superiors talking down to subordinates. Open OCC is marked by reciprocity—the openness and honesty within the relationship; feedback perceptiveness—sensitivity of supervisors to feedback; feedback responsiveness—the degree to which a supervisor gives feedback to subordinate requests or grievances; and feedback permissiveness—the degree to which supervisors permit and encourage feedback from subordinates (Gibb 1961).

Essential to a positive OCC is communication openness, information adequacy, and communication supportiveness. When information is open, employees have a grasp of what is happening in the organization. If an organization is open, adequate information is available for all employees. When leaders keep employees in the loop, they are being supportive. When leaders leave employees out of the loop because of lack of trust or power hoarding, they are being defensive. Defensive behaviors are not conducive to building a positive OCC. Managers have the critical role in the communication process of keeping everyone informed. Executive management must empower, engage, and enable their subordinates to communicate and direct the flow of information in the organization. The open and supportive OCC model presented in Figure 3.1 shows that

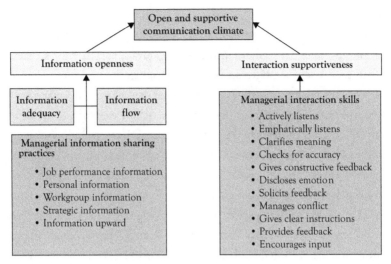

Figure 3.1 *Comprehensive organizational communication climate model*

Source: Robertson (2003, p. 32).

information must flow smoothly between all levels of the organization and across functional areas (Robertson 2003).

Potential traps exist for leaders in interpersonal communications between the manager and the employees, especially when the relationship is new. The best way for the executive to avoid the traps that result from failed leadership is to establish positive impressions with employees from the very beginning. Research has indicated that trust and commitment do not just happen automatically, but rather that they are forged and maintained by managers communicating effectively (Appelbaum et al. 2013).

At times, it may be necessary to reshape some of the networks that have developed in a firm in order to have a better OCC. Changing the OCC within a firm is not easy, and the ease of changing it depends on the number of subgroups or silos within the organization. You may also find that the structure of these silos differs because of the various types of work that occur within them. While workers communicate one way within their group, they may need to learn how to communicate effectively with other groups.

It is vital that managers know how information flows in the organization. An organization chart by design unintentionally promotes the formation of silos within the organization and impedes the flow of communication between functional areas. The need to facilitate communication increases with more involved organizational structures. Some organizations do not have an organization chart in an effort to enable employees to communicate with whomever they need. The Japanese developed what is known as the quality circle, where everyone is equal and can talk to other individuals no matter what their level is within the organization. Examining the organization chart and considering the limitations it may inadvertently put on the employees is important to communication strategy. If the chart is making managing too bureaucratic, then a change may be necessary. You can use the model in Figure 3.1 as a self-help tool to become a more effective manager. Frequently, employees speak past one another cross-functionally because their working vocabularies are different. Learning the language of other functional areas takes time because departmental employees often have limited knowledge of what happens in the rest of the company. However, this lack of understanding decreases when employees listen, ask questions, and learn to rephrase technical information so that others can understand it. Working in cross-functional teams helps to open lines of communication across the organization.

In an organization with a supportive communication climate, its members write and speak descriptive messages that are clear and specific without judgmental statements or words. In a supportive communication climate, problems will be posed as mutual problems to be worked on, communication will be open and honest in spontaneous messages, employees at all levels will be empathetic to the feelings and thoughts of others, messages will indicate an equality of worth between all levels of employees, and point-of-view messages will be posited as provisional and open to investigation. If an organization is not supportive, the climate will be defensive and not conducive to effective communication.

Supportive communication requires the ability to communicate and manage attitudes as well as information. Organizations can benefit from an examination of managers at all levels concerning their experience, judgment, intelligence, relationships, and insights, and then design training programs that help managers become better communicators. This may mean looking at "who does what," "where is it done," and "how is it done."

OCC starts with the CEO and board of directors and extends throughout the levels of management. Many managers are not only dealing with people in their home country but also with employees, customers, or suppliers in other countries. They may be virtually supervising employees from other nations and cultures. Employees with different cultural backgrounds can also find it difficult to assimilate into the existing organization. It is necessary that their managers spend time learning about their cultural differences and helping the person feel like a part of the overall organization. The Window into Practical Reality 3.2 exemplifies how poor OCC can be detrimental to business success.

Window into Practical Reality 3.2

The Rise and Fall of a Titan

CBS News reported on February 9, 2005, that Hewlett-Packard's (HP's) board of directors had fired Carly Fiorina after a 6-year reign as CEO. Fiorina's power-driven move to acquire Compaq was seen as too risky by many, and some charged her with inability to hear her constituents. This cited communication failure led to covert rebellion among the ranks and resulted in a very poor OCC during much of Fiorina's reign. The board accused Fiorina of failing to execute the planned strategy. She also had a strained relationship with the son of one of HP's late cofounders, HP director Walter Hewlett who openly opposed the Compaq acquisition because he felt it was overpriced.

The problem was probably not so much that Fiorina did not perform as the board of directors expected, but that she would not or could not hear her dissenters' concerns. Media reported that Fiorina's drive to acquire Compaq interfered with her managerial interaction skills (Vries 2005).

Using the complete OCC model shown in Figure 3.1, can you identify some of the skills that Fiorina obviously used to climb to the top of HP's hierarchy to become its CEO? Conversely, can you use the model to describe how her violating of these fundamentals led to her inevitable ouster?

As an organization grows, it generally will add departments and divisions, making communication connections grow exponentially. As a firm grows, the individuals joining the organization are likely to be more diverse, which leads to managers having to learn about their employees' differences and how they communicate. These differences could be due to their ethnic background, native language, gender, or anything else that differentiates people. As a firm grows, the management must also consider new ways to organize processes.

External stakeholders gauge the organization's communication climate by media messages and the way that customers and employees talk about the firm. A firm's external prestige is a direct result of employees' buy-in to the goals, values, and achievements of the organization. The communication climate affects how employees identify with the firm and project their impressions externally.

Culture

Subordinates can undermine managerial authority. Failing to understand the cultural forces at play can jeopardize managerial authority and ultimately impact the bottom line (Manzoni and Barsoux 2009). When managers do not have knowledge of organizational culture, it is impossible for them to change a traditional, rigid organization of yesterday into one that is flexible and evolving for tomorrow (Flannery, Hofrichter, and Platten 1996).

Very little was written on *corporate culture* prior to 1979 (Kotter and Heskett 1992). More recently, there has been a great deal of research on corporate culture. Studies have addressed how leaders should examine the artifacts, espoused values, and basic underlying assumptions as layers of organizational culture. What is clear is the strong influence managerial communication (MC) has on shaping corporate culture by steering the entire direction of the organization toward prosperity or ruin.

The common managerial practice of attempting to decentralize decision making prior to assessing meaning in culture is not recommended. Attempts to change organizational culture cannot resolve business problems when there is incomplete knowledge of the current organizational culture. Changes in culture must accompany changes in values, beliefs, and core assumptions.

Even though an adaptive culture cannot account for 100 percent of corporate performance, developing successful strategies to deliver value to major constituencies is very important. Culture can be either the brakes or the fuel for the engine of success of an organization and is just as important as the primary functions of finance and information technology (Rigsby and Greco 2003). Organizational culture influences employees' perspectives, just as societal cultural shapes citizens. Individuals learn their societal culture and share their culture first with their family and then with the broader community in which they live. To disseminate the culture, the existing members must share their beliefs and values with the next generation or newcomers, so that the new members understand what is required to be a member of the culture. Business culture is learned in much the same way as is societal culture.

Established Layers of Culture

Weick (2001) argues that meaning is distinct from decision making by asserting that meaning precedes decision making. He argues that managers must understand the nature of what is happening before they can decide on what to do about it. His assessment is that even though centralized and decentralized authority are both valuable in certain situations, understanding culture can make decentralized decision making more desirable. Being in the loop as culture is forming, reforming, and affecting outcomes is a way for top management to effectively gauge, anticipate, and dislodge the potential hazards of unhealthy communications (both symbolic and explicit), resulting in organizational cultures that go awry. Corporate culture can drive performance and the core values that comprise corporate culture. The meaning and interpretation of organization and corporate culture content can be broad, spanning all tiers and functions of management.

Other theorists have offered additional definitions essential to the consideration of organizational culture. Schein (1992) stated that (1) *artifacts* are all the phenomena that are visible, (2) *espoused values* are confirmed by shared social experiences of group members and this layer of conscious culture can be used to predict much of the behavior that can be observed at the artifactual level, and (3) *basic underlying assumptions* become embedded in culture when solutions to group problems work repeatedly.

Similarly, Trompenaars and Hampden-Turner (1998) stated that the (1) *outer layer* is explicit products that are the observable reality of the culture such as food, language, or shrines; (2) the *middle layers* are norms and a mutual sense of a group's right and wrong, and values are those beliefs that determine or define what the group might think is good and bad; and (3) *the core* is made of assumptions about existence, which are implicit to the members of the culture to increase people's effectiveness at solving problems.

Shared meanings are man-made and transcend the people in the culture. The more visible the culture, the easier it is to change; the less visible the culture, the more resistant it is to change. A good example of the reason artifacts, the observable most visible reality of the culture, matter in shared meanings is shown in the Window into Practical Reality 3.3.

Window into Practical Reality 3.3

Books on Shelves, Diplomas, and Awards Displayed on Walls Matter!

Every year the college professors are assembled together to receive annual teaching awards based on student surveys and student nominations. Input from department heads are also considered in which faculty members would receive the three awards, one for each department in the college. There is often a $2,000 cash prize associated with the award.

In addition to teaching and research, faculty in the particular college are required to advise students on their course selections, career interests, and any other subjects relating to the students' success. One assistant professor is respected in the college, and has had some significant articles published in her field of finance, which has garnered her some respect in the field. Nonetheless, she has not received a teaching award. Moreover, the college of business has very few female faculty, and this assistant professor is the only one teaching finance at both the graduate and undergraduate levels.

The finance professor is always available in her office during office hours and is willing to meet any of her students by appointment too. She has had no complaints from any students on any serious matter. The assistant professor conveys her concerns with a colleague in the college who is a full professor in the management area about her desire to receive the award, especially since she is up for tenure in just 1 year. The full professor of management asked the assistant professor of finance a very interesting question.

He asked, "What does your office look like?"

She answers, "About the same as it did when I moved in."

He replied, "That was about five years ago, correct?"

She replied, "Yes, just about."

The full professor tells the assistant professor, "Do you think it is about time that you dust off some of your books, diplomas, and awards and move them into your office space? Students care about these things." He continues, "apparently your office does not reflect to your students who you are really." The assistant professor spent some money on having her three college diplomas, including her PhD degree, framed and hung them on her office walls. She relocated about 200 of her books, many of which she had been collecting since high school from her home office. She also posted in plain sight three framed awards that she had received from finance conferences she attended over the years.

When students visited her office, a frequent question to her was, "Wow! Did you read all these books?!" The assistant professor of finance proudly declared, "Yes, I did," to any student who asked. The very next semester, many students nominated the assistant professor for the teaching award, and she received the teaching award right in time for her tenure application.

- Do you suspect that when the assistant professor of finance changed the artifacts in her office space that she changed the shared meaning in the culture among students in the college of business?
- Was it merely a coincidence that she received the award for the first time after she hung the diplomas and awards and moved a lot of books into her office space?

Formal and Informal Networks

Studies have shown that performance increases when the CEO and marketing vice president share the same vision and communicate that vision vertically to the rest of the firm. How to share that vision vertically; however, is not always clear. Top management must obviously communicate adequately with the functional managers, and the functional managers must communicate with their subordinates. Maintaining an organizational structure which promotes effective vertical communication of a company's vision requires formal processes.

Formal Networks

The communication structure of an organization is both formal and informal. The more formal the structure, the more messages have to follow channels depicted in the formal organization chart of the company; the more informal the structure, the easier it is to go directly to the person with whom you wish to communicate.

In very *formal networks*, information moves down the depicted lines of authority, and employees do not bypass their bosses when communicating with others in the organization. The employee communicates upward through the direct supervisor, who then will send the message up the chain of command. Certain information is typically communicated more formally, such as common rules, regulations, standard operating procedures, plans, schedules, and forecasts. A formal organizational structure will often require that written channels of communication be used for formalized decision making. Coordination must exist between the different groups within the organization in order to accomplish the overall goals of the organization.

Katz and Kahn (1966) are credited with identifying the three directions of communication flow: communications down the line—down to the workers; horizontal communications—between departments; and communication upward—up toward top management.

Upward communication is used to keep management informed. Upward communication may happen through reports, meetings, or informal communications. If top management encourages upward communication, a company's leadership is more likely to learn about the concerns and suggestions that employees have.

Downward communication is generally used to instruct workers, build and maintain the morale and goodwill of the workers, keep routine and special activities moving smoothly and efficiently, and to encourage upward communication. Employees want guidelines and information from management, and management wants input and feedback from employees.

Horizontal (lateral) communication strengthens interpersonal relationships across departments and units within the company. Such an exchange helps to minimize conflict, promote understanding, and increase coordination between departments or units. Getting others to communicate their needs is a two-way process and generally starts with how managers encourage and motivate their employees. It is helpful for managers to start conversations by sharing their skills and knowledge and empowering the employees to do the same.

Some organizations have a culture of everyone being allowed to communicate with anyone in the firm, at any level. Other organizations want communication to travel along established routes—subordinate to supervisor to superior. Of course, in the first type of culture, it is very easy to quickly let people at the top know what is happening and vice versa; however, people in the middle may be left out. The use of e-mail has increased broad awareness in many organizations, as messages can be copied to multiple recipients simultaneously.

Given that organizations often make strategic changes due to internal or external pressures, top managers must skillfully use ways to quickly communicate vertically to multiple recipients throughout the firm. Managers at all levels must help to build everyone's understanding, an identity with the company, and commitment to the strategy's formulation, dissemination, and implementation. It is also necessary that top management encourage and actually listen to responses from those at varying levels in the organization.

Informal Networks

In more *informal networks*, everyone can communicate directly with everyone else. You would still need to keep your boss informed of what you are doing, but there is no pressure on you to only tell your boss.

The formality or informality of an organization generally starts at the top and depends upon the technical, political, and economic environment of the organization. You will find organizations such as Microsoft that are very informal and organizations such as General Motors that are more formalized.

Much of an organization's communication takes place through informal processes. Therefore, key linkages are essential. These linkages between the areas of the firm determine the frequency of communication: Who receives the communication, and whether the meaning of the communication is shared. Informal communication networks are like spiderwebs because various areas are interconnected no matter how far they are from the top. Frequent communication between the functional areas and top management will impact both functional and organizational performance. If a firm does not have shared understanding, there will be barriers to successful strategic plan implementation (Rapert, Velliquette, and Garretson 2002).

The grapevine is a form of informal communication. With Twitter and other social media, jamming, texting, e-mail, and other technology, it is easy for information to be passed around a company very quickly. Gossip being transferred only at the water fountain is a thing of the past. What makes grapevines important to managers is that they typically carry more information than formal networks. While the grapevine may distribute gossip, rumors, and half-truths, it also frequently provides accurate information. This information can be useful to managers, who should know how and when to use the grapevine.

What makes individuals pass on certain information, yet desire other information? Typically, this decision is based on the salience or importance of the information to the individual, the effect of the channel chosen, and the cultural norms of the organization. Johnson and others (1994) found that employees use informal channels more than formal channels in business. Roles tend to dictate the number of formal and informal communication channels that are used. Also, employees scrutinize formal communication for characteristics such as editorial tone more than they do with information from informal channels.

Figure 3.2 shows how important it is for managers to dial into the other jobs employees do, in addition to their formal assignments (Bell

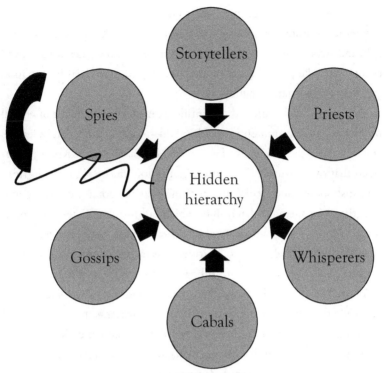

Figure 3.2 Cultural network of the hidden hierarchy

2009). It is essential that you as a manager know the quality of the communications radiating from the hidden hierarchy. The phone connected directly to the hidden hierarchy in Figure 3.2 is a visual reminder to managers of the importance of being in the loop of informal corporate cultural communications.

Deal and Kennedy (1982) created the metaphors of spies, storytellers, priests, whisperers, cabals, and gossips to describe the various types of communication activities occurring in the cultural network of the hidden hierarchy. These metaphors describe each of the other jobs people do at work within a MC context. *Spies* are people who are loyal in the network and those who keep others informed of what is going on. A *storyteller* is a person who can change reality by interpreting what goes on in a company to suit their own perception. *Priests* tend to be worriers, responsible for guarding the company's values and keeping the flock together. *Whisperers* work like Machiavelli from behind the throne, but without a formal portfolio—the source of their power is the boss's ear. *Cabals* plot a common purpose by joining together in unions that provide personal gain and advancement. *Gossips* will name names, know dates, salaries, and events that take place, and they carry the day-to-day trivial information cautiously appreciated by most.

Values and styles affect the identification and management of ethical problems, causing unintentional ethical dilemmas. Unfortunately, leaders are sometimes the architects of negative cultures. Dent and Krefft (2004) assert that two cultures exist in any organization, the one that results from fear, dishonesty, and denial and the one that invigorates creativity and integrity. Management determines which culture dominates. Organizational cultures are paradoxical because they contain both productive and counterproductive elements of culture. This factor helps explain why the bankers played hot potato with subprime mortgages, even though nearly every executive knew the risks. Questions emerge as to why some bankers behaved ethically while others did not: What elements in some financial institutions' cultures steered them toward fortitude amid the subprime lending free-for-all, and what elements in other financial institutions' cultures steered them toward depravity (falsifying documents, hiding audit documents from the Securities and Exchange Commission [SEC], repackaging bad debt, ostracizing whistle-blowers and those refusing to violate the law, policy, and procedure, and so on)?

Summary

Leadership is the process of providing forward movement for the organization and vision for the future. Leaders strive to achieve common goals for the common good. Power can be used for the common good or for selfish purposes. Six bases of power are referent power, expert power, legitimate power, reward power, coercive power, and the leader—member exchange. The OCC is determined by the degree of openness, trust, confidence, participation in decision making, and acceptance. OCC comprises both actions and attitudes and is highly influenced by how supervisors define their roles and the roles of subordinates within the firm.

The layers of culture include (1) artifacts, the most visible layer that contains all the phenomena that can be seen, heard, or felt when a person first encounters a new group with an unfamiliar culture; (2) espoused values, which are confirmed by shared social experiences of group members that can be used to predict much of the behavior observable at the artifactual level; and (3) basic underlying assumptions, which become embedded in a culture when solutions to group problems work repeatedly.

The three directions of communication flow are down the line communication that originates with managers and is directed down to the workers; horizontal communication that occurs between members of different lateral departments; and upward communication that begins with employees and moves up toward top management.

In a company with a formal communication structure, employees avoid bypassing their bosses when communicating with others in the organization. In formal communication, an employee always tells the direct supervisor, who then will send the message up the chain of command. In informal organizations, everyone can communicate directly with everyone else. The grapevine is a form of informal communication that managers can use to their advantage. Technology facilitates the easy and fast movement of information around a company.

CHAPTER 4

Ethical Issues in Management Communication

Objectives

After reading this chapter, you will be able to:

1. define the theories of moral problems in business;
2. explain how moral philosophy develops;
3. differentiate between personal ethics and societal ethics;
4. identify ethical issues in lieu of codes of ethics;
5. determine appropriate situations for whistleblowing;
6. explain the guidelines for ethical behavior.

Introduction

If people are to work together successfully, they must agree to share common customs and standards of conduct. If they cannot agree on the tenets of ethical conduct, there will be no consensus on the organization's behaviors. Many would defend the right of a sovereign society to govern itself. Therefore, the tenets of ethical conduct a society chooses for itself will inevitably spillover into the business environments. Bad choices by society are bad for business.

Unethical decisions are made all the time: Why does this happen? People steal, not only for themselves but also for their company. Power, greed, and misplaced values are the major causes of unethical decisions in business. The 2008 U.S. financial crisis was due in large part to the unethical decisions made by Fannie Mae leaders Franklin Raines, CEO and Chairman, and Tim Howard, CFO. They told banks to make loans to unqualified people. They manipulated the earnings to trigger bonuses for themselves. The profit motive drove them to make bad decisions. When people in an organization learn that their leaders are dishonest, the credibility of those leaders is destroyed.

Ethical issues that are very important for managerial communication effectiveness today include social responsibility, dealing with conflict of interest, payoffs, financial results, product safety, liability, whistleblowing, organizational politics, training and development, ambivalence, bribery, and quid pro quo.

Moral Problems Common to Business

Philosophers over several centuries developed theories to explain how people respond to the ethical problems that societies face.

Consequentialism

Consequentialism results when the profit motive or the success of the business supersedes the duty to do what is right for society. In fact, this theory could explain the ethical breaches of many businesses. A recipe for trouble can occur when the results are considered to be more important than duty to society, to not cause harm, or to obey the federal and state laws that protect consumers and the public. If there is an opportunity for impropriety, then the choice made requires the person to act according to an established code.

Decision Theory

Codes of ethics are justified by *decision theory* that applies when there is limited information to make a rational choice or to achieve an outcome that is optimal. These codes provide guidelines for acceptable actions. Some professionals refer to *decision theory* as the "sniff test." The code should be applied to ethical situations to be sure that it is functional. If there is a code of ethics, all employees should have a copy and should be given instructions on its use. Top management must also use the code, if it is to be effective at lower levels in the organization. The code should also include guidelines concerning punishments for violations.

Deontology

Deontology refers to judging the morality of an action on that action's adherence to rules. Managers must effectively communicate ethical standards in order for employees to incorporate those values into the organizational culture. However, deontology is concerned with a person feeling more concern for doing his or her duty than worrying about any potential harm his or her actions will cause to others. Managers are an essential corporate tool for communicating ethical values. Fraud and misconduct often occur when duty to a company becomes more important than the consequences to society.

Teleology

Teleology is the notion that the universe has a purpose and that purpose is often prescribed by a divine being. Many people believe that there is one God, the Supreme Being, whose will provides the purpose to human existence. According to Bell and others (2011) the strongest predictions of ethical behavior are the family (upbringing), friends, and beliefs that are generally stronger than the company's values and beliefs.

Truett Cathy's personal ethics shaped the moral code of Chick-fil-A, a company he founded in 1946, when he decided not to operate the first restaurant he opened in Hapeville, Georgia, on Sundays. Cathy had a firm belief that employees should be able to worship, be with family and friends, and get some rest on Sunday. Today thousands of Chick-fil-A restaurants currently operate in the United States, and each of them forgoes hundreds of thousands of dollars in revenues by closing their doors on Sundays. At Chick-fil-A, adhering to the founder's personal ethics, is more important than making money on Sundays. Recently, *Business Insider's* Kate Taylor (2018) reported that Gen Zers have a passion for Chick-fil-A. It is no wonder that the average annual per restaurant sales is $4.4 million, compared to KFC's $1.1 million per restaurant sales for the same period. Chick-Fil-A continues to be closed on Sundays, yet its revenues for all stores in 2017 was $9 billion, up from $8 billion in 2016. Chick-Fil-A is evidence that teleological beliefs can be integrated into the modern capital structure as intense competition against fast-food chains owned and operated by conglomerates. Window into Practical Reality 4.1 presents a sobering example of persistent challenges to teleological ethics that played out in the Supreme Court of the United States (SCOTUS) when Hobby Lobby sued the federal government.

Window into Practical Reality 4.1

SCOTUS Rules in Favor of Hobby Lobby

In 2012, Hobby Lobby sued Kathleen Sebelius, the then head of Department of Health and Human Services (HHS) on the grounds that the company was being forced to violate its owners' religious beliefs to provide abortion related health care to its employees. In the 2014 ruling, the Supreme Court of the United States (SCOTUS) ruled against the Obama Administration, in favor of David and Barbara Green, owners of the privately held business. The court rules that the owners of Hobby Lobby *did not* have to violate their faith; moreover, the Green family *should not* be forced to pay fines for not following rules laid down by HHS relating to contraception drugs.

According to SCOTUS, the Affordable Health Care Act ("Obama Care") regulations presented a substantial violation and burden to the religious beliefs of the Greens, a clear violation of the *Religious Freedom Restoration Act (RFRA) of 1993*. The RFRA protects people who have sincere religious beliefs which they demonstrate by routine practice of their faith. Under RFRA, Americans are not required to abide by any law that substantially puts a burden on the free exercise of their religious beliefs.

SCOTUS agreed with the main issues of the Green's argument, and in this case, religious freedom prevailed over secular laws. The pivotal issue was that the HHS mandate would have required Hobby Lobby to provide and facilitate drugs that would terminate the lives of unborn children whose mothers were covered on its insurance plan. Clearly, providing such a plan was a violation of the Green family's righteous values. In opposition, many who are secularists believe state powers should not be hindered or interfered with by religious beliefs, irrespective of the faith or denomination. This lawsuit exemplified the battle between the modern feminist belief "that a woman's body is her own" and a religious doctrinal belief structure rooted in the command- ment "Thou shalt not kill." Women can have abortions, the court de- termined, but Hobby Lobby does not have to pay for it.

- Do you believe the Greens were able to prevail in court simply because they had an estimated wealth of over $1 billion?
- Was the Green family wrong in filing the lawsuit against HHS because their religion makes them bigots?
- If you are a woman of childbearing age, would you work for Hobby Lobby? Why or why not?
- Are more cases like this likely in the future?

Utilitarianism

Utilitarianism theory supports making decisions based on the greatest amount of pleasure and the least amount of pain for the greatest number of people; in other words, actions should improve the human experience in mass. Many of the moral problems to which utilitarianism is applied are broadly societal, rather than applications to businesses as regulatory mandates.

The United States has historically been a society of competing ethi- cal beliefs. In the absence of agreements or consensus on what behavior ought to be acceptable in society, historically its citizens have had violent conflicts that have sometimes lasted for decades. Examples of contested societal ethics are legalized slavery, alcohol prohibition, voter I.D. laws, prohibition against women's voting, and Jim Crow (separate but equal) laws. For every proponent of these types of laws, there was an unrelenting opponent whose belief in the unrighteousness of such laws was intractable.

Society has imposed many of its societal values through laws and regulations on business operations and activities. In the United States, federal, state, county, and city governments regulate the societal ethics that are imposed on businesses, including equal protection and affirma- tive action laws. Some states imposed antimiscegenation laws until the Supreme Court struck them down in 1967 as described in the Window into Practical Reality 4.2.

Window into Practical Reality 4.2

Loving vs. Virginia, 388 U.S. 1 (1967)

Loving vs. Virginia was a landmark U.S. Supreme Court ruling handed down in 1967 that marked a milestone in civil rights. The U.S. Supreme Court unanimously decided that Virginia's antimiscegenation statute, the Racial Integrity Act of 1924, was unconstitutional. The ruling overturned the *Pace vs. Alabama* law of 1883, which ended the societal practice of recognizing only marriages between people deemed to be of the same race. This decision that ended laws against interracial unions in the United States took decades to happen and reflected both deontological ethics and utilitarianism thinking.

Despite the outcry from proponents of these laws, the Supreme Court's decision seemed to be predicated more on duty to the entire U.S. society, despite the expected immediate consequences of hate crimes and violence against black Americans as a result of the decision. For many younger U.S. citizens, it is hard to imagine that such laws have existed in recent history.

How has the Supreme Court's decision to strike down antimiscegenation statutes resulted in a greater (utilitarian) good for U.S. citizens as a whole?

Equal protection laws are essential in helping to root out racism, sexism, and ageism in the workplace, so that all U.S. citizens will have a better opportunity to prosper and advance in their careers. The need for such laws is a testament to the fact that personal values of hate and discrimination spillover into the workplace. They also reflect a utilitarian intention in regulating all U.S. businesses to ensure certain types of moral conduct in the workplace.

A recent study of MBA students by Zaremba (2000) found that the students' value systems varied widely. When the students discussed these differences, many were shocked to learn that people they were working with had such different values from their own. The majority of the students believed that if a statement was not prefaced with the qualifying statement "this is the truth," the receiver of the message was obligated to discover if the statement was in fact true.

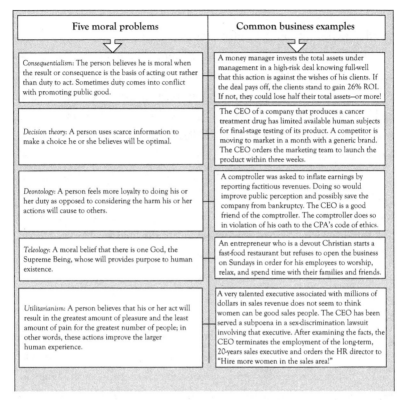

Five moral problems	Common business examples
Consequentialism: The person believes he is moral when the result or consequence is the basis of acting out rather than duty to act. Sometimes duty comes into conflict with promoting public good.	A money manager invests the total assets under management in a high-risk deal knowing full-well that this action is against the wishes of his clients. If the deal pays off, the clients stand to gain 26% ROI. If not, they could lose half their total assets—or more!
Decision theory: A person uses scarce information to make a choice he or she believes will be optimal.	The CEO of a company that produces a cancer treatment drug has limited available human subjects for final-stage testing of its product. A competitor is moving to market in a month with a generic brand. The CEO orders the marketing team to launch the product within three weeks.
Deontology: A person feels more loyalty to doing his or her duty as opposed to considering the harm his or her actions will cause to others.	A comptroller was asked to inflate earnings by reporting factitious revenues. Doing so would improve public perception and possibly save the company from bankruptcy. The CEO is a good friend of the comptroller. The comptroller does so in violation of his oath to the CPA's code of ethics.
Teleology: A moral belief that there is one God, the Supreme Being, whose will provides purpose to human existence.	An entrepreneur who is a devout Christian starts a fast-food restaurant but refuses to open the business on Sundays in order for his employees to worship, relax, and spend time with their families and friends.
Utilitarianism: A person believes that his or her act will result in the greatest amount of pleasure and the least amount of pain for the greatest number of people; in other words, these actions improve the larger human experience.	A very talented executive associated with millions of dollars in sales revenue does not seem to think women can be good sales people. The CEO has been served a subpoena in a sex-discrimination lawsuit involving that executive. After examining the facts, the CEO terminates the employment of the long-term, 20-years sales executive and orders the HR director to "Hire more women in the sales area!"

Figure 4.1 Five theories of moral problems common to the business environment

Source: Feinberg (1996).

Figure 4.1 illustrates moral problems and some hypothetical examples of why consequentialism, decision theory, deontology, teleology, and utilitarianism present moral challenges to business. Managers encounter a broad range of decisions daily, where their choices can be detrimental to thousands, if not millions, of people.

The Central Issues of Moral Philosophy

The Greek word *philosophy* literally means the love of wisdom. Arguably, Socrates was sincere in his pursuit of wisdom. To Socrates, the question was not so much "What is?" but "What ought to be?" Socrates stated that "the unexamined life is not worth living." *Egoism* is the ability to determine and do what is best for yourself; *altruism* is the ability to understand how your actions will affect others.

There are three main branches of Western philosophy: *epistemology*—a view that humans can know about the world in which they exist, thus, people pursue answers to questions concerning phenomenon that can be tested and verified or refuted; *metaphysics*—a view that knowledge can be gained from abstraction (including religious beliefs); and *ethics*—a view of right and wrong conduct affecting others' welfare.

As one of three main branches of Western philosophy, ethics has been examined for many centuries. Unalienable right bestowed by God for individuals are guaranteed by the Constitution of the United States. These rights include equal protection under the laws for free speech and a free press, a right to remain silent, and freedom of religion. Rights such as these are the basis of U.S. citizens societal ethics of these tenets are a culmination of centuries of Western philosophy. Societies, however, have embraced ethics differently.

When Socrates was alive, the Greeks worshiped many gods. Socrates routinely asked troubling questions concerning this belief system like: "What happens when two gods of equal strength and power disagree?" When people's common beliefs cannot resolve their ethical dilemmas, people become frustrated and feel threatened. Socrates asked the Athenians so many poignant questions that his challenging ideas led to a saucer of hemlock that sent him to his grave. Values and beliefs are profound for individuals. Ordinary people, in situations where they feel a need to reflect consciously on decisions they honestly cannot determine immediately to be right or wrong, are in fact searching for wisdom.

Moral philosophy is the outcome of a process through which individuals reflect consciously on the precepts that govern their ordinary habits of moral choice. Reflection is required when precepts about what is right and wrong can no longer enable the person to automatically resolve ethical dilemmas. With old values believed to be insufficient to aid in resolving the moral problem, a conscious reflection on those values is required of the individual. It is through this process of conscious reflection that an individual is elevated to a higher level of ethics called moral philosophy. Theologians, philosophers, and academicians alike have struggled for centuries to understand and explain these types of moral decisions. Ethical decision making is predicated on the values and beliefs that influence the philosophy supporting an individual's or culture's moral code. Therefore, values and ethics are both personal and societal.

The base of ethical judgments is the sense of right or wrong. A judgment based on what is easiest, best, or most effective in achieving an objective is based on practical ethics. Subjective judgments are measured by degrees rather than by absolutes of what is ethical or unethical in a society (Lewicki, Saunders, and Minton 2007). Business morality consists of doing one's duty, despite concern for the probable outcomes of such choices. Individuals may at times perceive that their duty to their company is more important than the common good for society.

Employees usually learn more about a particular company's ethical values from fellow employees rather than from their supervisors. This reality indicates that managers should be more proactive in having discussions about ethical issues with employees. Employees can also learn company ethical values through training and orientation programs as well as from handbooks. The best ethical codes are the ones that employees intuitively act upon, making it important that values are interwoven throughout the organization's culture. Adding many cultures to the mix makes understanding ethics even more complex. The constraints when dealing with an ethical dilemma include international and domestic laws, internal or industry codes of ethics, the interest of the stakeholders, and personal values.

Many global business managers rely on *hypernorms* today, which are the transnational norms forming across cultures. The hypernorm would say that bribery is wrong, although there are countries where bribery is practiced. Proponents of globalization generally would like to have all employees follow the same values and beliefs around the globe; though this is not always possible, due to varying cultural and societal values and beliefs. Examples of current hypernorms are global standard accounting practices, international regulations for the movement of goods, and international safety standards.

Four approaches for working with ethics internationally include the foreign-country approach, empire approach, interconnection approach, and global approach. In the *foreign-country approach,* the organization conforms to the ethics of the host country. In the *empire approach,* home-based ethics are applied in the host situation. The *interconnection approach* considers the needs of both groups that are interacting. The *global approach* looks at what is good for the world, rather than the local ethical customs (Donaldson and Dunfee 1999).

Each of these methods has its challenges. With the foreign-country approach, the company has no oversight or restraints on the host country's ethics; while the empire approach, does not take into account the cultural and personal values of those in the host country. Trying to balance multiple interests is challenging at best, when applying the interconnection or global approaches, though the rewards are great when efforts are successful.

Personal and Societal Ethics

There are distinctions between definitions of the terms personal values, personal ethics, societal values, and societal ethics, although they are interdependent. *Personal values* are the individual's trusted, closely held beliefs; *personal ethics* refers to an individual's philosophy that serves as a moral code of conduct. On the other hand, *societal values* are the trusted and closely held beliefs imposed on the individual by the society in which he or she lives. *Societal ethics* is the totality of individual philosophies that culminate in a systematic moral code of conduct agreed on by members of a society.

Ethics in business includes the rules, standards, principles, or codes that give the members of a firm a moral compass for determining the correct behavior in specific situations. The degree of accountability affects people's ethical behaviors. The stronger a personal relationship is, the more unlikely unethical behavior will be. Workers solve ethical dilemmas based on their culture, their individual beliefs (based on the ethical choices), the work situation, and the relationships they have with other workers. Role systems theory has shown that firm accountability expectations and the consequences of noncompliance are important keys regarding the choices employees will make.

Our ethical beliefs follow us to the workplace. Because of immigration from all over the world, there are probably more ethical differences between individuals in the United States than anywhere else in the world. Originally, immigration was mainly from Europe and Africa, but now it has a broader base. Additionally, globalization of organizations involves the consideration of different ethical belief standards around the world. It is not enough to speak the same language. We also need to understand what the others believe, if we are to trust them to carry out the goals of the firm.

Conflicting values between workers are not unusual. Some workers will believe they are to simply obey authority no matter what the consequences might be. Other workers will believe they should question orders if something does not appear to be correct. When company and personal values clash, individuals will ask themselves who they owe loyalty to first—themselves or the company. For many people, the conflict with their loyalty to family and family beliefs may also be problematic. For others, societal concerns may be more important than company goals. A good example of personal ethics vis-a-vis societal ethics is presented in Window into Practical Reality 4.3.

Window into Practical Reality 4.3

The Personal Ethics of the "Far Right" vs. Societal Ethics of the "Far Left"

There is a rift in the American culture which stems from personal ethics of religious beliefs versus societal ethics drawn from secular culture. People on the "far right" are commonly referred to in the media as religious zealots. On the other hand, people on the "far left" are referred to as Social Justice Warriors (SJWs) by alternative media sources, mostly existing on the internet. *Secularism* is the sincere belief that the church should be completely separate from the state. The clash between secular values and religious values lead to conflicts of ethics. Fornication, sex before marriage, has become acceptable in the secular culture but continues to be frowned upon by people who hold extreme religious views. The King James Version of the New Testament Bible, Romans 1:29 prohibits: *Being filled with all unrighteousness, fornication, wickedness, covetousness, maliciousness; full of envy, murder, debate, deceit, malignity; whisperers . . .*

A backlash response to the broad acceptance of men engaging in promiscuous sex is the *SlutWalk*. Feminists believe that men hypocritically "slut-shame" women, thus, women should not be ashamed of their own promiscuous behaviors. However, when a large number of unmarried women and teenagers have children, the cost to taxpayers can be staggering.

According to The National Vital Statistics Reports (Martin et al. 2018), black teenagers ages 15 to 19, gave birth to 41,780 out of 389,780 live births accounting for 10.7 percent of black babies born in 2016; 97.5 percent of teens were unmarried. A similar statistic is true for Hispanic teenagers 15 to 19, who gave birth to 66,219 out of 483,527 live births, accounting for 13.7 percent of Hispanic babies born in 2016; 88.5 percent of teens were unmarried. For all races, 89.1 percent of teenagers 15 to 19 were unmarried, bringing into the world 186,981 babies out of 1,569,796 children for all unmarried women in 2016. The marriage rate for people ages 25 to 34 has plummeted from 70 percent in 1965 to 50 percent in 2010. What's more, if the trend continues, the marriage rate would be zero by 2034. Fewer marriages mean more poor babies, and the odds that a child will be poor if born into a single parent household is 71 percent (Kotlikoff and Burns 2012).

In 2010, Congress allocated $927 billion to federal and state social programs, 40 percent of which went directly to cash, food, and housing assistance. "Roughly half of this welfare assistance, or $462 billion went to families with children, most of which are headed by single parents" (Wikipedia 2018). The state, in the vast majority of these cases, will provide the single mothers with a menu of public assistance programs (e.g., WIC: Women, Infant and Children Food Program, SNAP, school lunch, Medicaid, Section 8 Housing [HUD], child-care assistance, and much more). In many cases, the suite of services available is more lucrative than if the single mother worked full-time.

- Is it ethical that the religious zealot who lives a constrained life should be made to share the burden of paying for the children of men and women who show little or no restraint in their own behaviors?
- Is it justified that state and federal laws often supersede the personal ethics of millions of its religious citizens?
- If there was no welfare system in place, would secularists show more restraints? Would SlutWalks be feasible without a welfare system in place?
- Given that marriage is rapidly declining, resulting in more single mothers, is the current federal spending on welfare entitlements sustainable?

When faced with conflicting personal and work values, an employee can either do nothing, quit, work to change the system, or blow the whistle. Part of the choice will depend on how the person sees the situation. Is it partially wrong or completely wrong? Is it a direct lie or a lie to buy time? Is it illegal or just wrong? Is it unsafe? Ethics can be thought of as a continuum from white to black, where many situations are in shades of gray. Some individuals see everything as one extreme or the other—either white or black. Most people see things as shades of gray based upon their ethical belief structure. Therefore, as a manager, it is important that your ethical and moral perceptions are in sync with those of your workers. The more the two agree, the easier it will be for you to work together. Rules that govern the conduct of ordinary people in any society, including organizations that exist within that society, can make ethical decision making even more complex. If your ethics are questionable, wrong ethical decisions may be made such as paying yourself a bonus when the company is losing money. Sometimes it is good for people to disagree so that hard questions are asked and answered.

Codes of Ethics

Situations involving questionable business ethics have been frequently in the news in recent years. The negative news and the aftermath of the situations have been devastating to many individuals, from a loss of retirement funds in U.S. companies to a loss of loved pets from contaminated pet food from China.

As we mature, we learn ethics and morals from those around us; ethics is very personal, cultural, and situational. Many professional organizations have attempted to govern the ethical conduct of their members, including these:

- American Bar Association Model Rules of Professional Conduct
- American Institute of Certified Public Accountants Code of Ethics (AICPA Code of Professional Conduct)
- American Nurses Association Code of Ethics
- National Commission for Health Education Credentialing, Inc. Code of Ethics
- National Society of Professional Engineers (NSPE Code of Ethics for Engineers)

The ethical codes of these organizations are believed to make it easier for their members to gauge what is and what is not acceptable conduct within the respective professions. For example, the code of conduct for judges requires them to recuse themselves from cases in which a conflict of interest could raise questions of reasonable doubt or impropriety. Many of these codes of conduct provide strict consequences for members who violate the codes, such as a certified public accountant (CPA) losing their license for insider trading. Often companies have formal ethical statements, which make it easier for an employee to determine how he or she will handle ethical situations and dilemmas. But in our global world, the problem of whose ethics or which ethical principles should be adopted is not an easy question to answer. Nevertheless, companies are in a serious position of figuring out how to respond to the perceived unethical atmosphere of business.

A research study found that 76 percent of workers had observed violations of the law or company policies during the prior 12 months. While nearly two-thirds of those surveyed did not feel that their company would discipline guilty employees, they also did not think that management even knew of the types of unethical behaviors that were occurring. In many cases, managers do not have enough information to make perfect decisions. Nevertheless, reporting wrongdoing is often predicated on urgency and devotion to doing what is perceived to be the right thing to do.

Appropriate Time for Whistleblowing

Whistleblowing has become more common in corporations and government in recent years. But how does an individual decide how and when to blow the whistle?

Ethical Dilemmas

Ethical dilemmas at work happen when people are asked to accept or do things which they know are illegal, immoral, or simply wrong. Lehman and Dufrene (2015, p. 10) list seven main reasons for illegal and unethical behavior which can stem from common causes:

- Excessive emphasis on profits
- Misplaced corporate loyalty
- Obsession with personal advancement

- Expectation of not getting caught
- Unethical tone set by top management
- Uncertainty about whether an action is wrong
- Unwillingness to take a stand for what is right.

Understanding the seven common causes of illegal and unethical behavior helps people in organizations develop a sensitivity to the signals of escalating pressure that can compromise an individual's values (Lehman and Dufrene 2015). It is always important for you to consider the position of others when communicating decisions that affect their work and personal life. *Put yourself in their shoes* and ask what you would want to know in their situation. Professional ethics is an evolving process of determining for ourselves what we believe to be right and wrong conduct, which includes values that combine to form our personal ethics. In some cases, whistleblowers are willing to end their careers (and in some cases their lives), to seek justice and punish wrongdoers for the greater good of society. Frequently, whistleblowing is the only option, when the individual is confronted with seeking justice against a large organization.

A good example of a whistleblowing dilemma is the situation in which top banks skipped the due diligence part of the home purchase and sales they financed. When sued by angry homeowners, banks produced fake documents created by document mills. Lynn Szymoniak, a fraud attorney foreclosed on by a big bank, who was also featured on the television show *60 Minutes*, won an $18 million share of a $95 million settlement after she blew the whistle on "robo-signing" fraud perpetuated by some of America's largest banks. Banks that lost crucial original assignment of mortgage documents hired teenagers to fraudulently create thousands of them. These documents were entered into court records as authentic, in some cases two years after the fact. Szymoniak researched 10,000 such documents and uncovered broad scale fraud perpetuated by the big banks (60 Minutes Overtime Staff 2012). Other forms of misconduct that might trigger whistleblowing include situations in which you witness bribes changing hands or kickbacks.

Kickbacks and Bribery

Decision theory is applicable to situations in which managers take or give kickbacks when they fear losing a deal, or when they believe that the practice is culturally necessary and acceptable. Managers may also engage in kickbacks and bribery when there is no real fear of getting caught.

Organizations like Baxter and General Motors (GM) have policies that forbid employees from taking gifts or gratuities from suppliers. Some companies require vendors to sign pledges that they will not engage in bribes or kickbacks to employees. Employees learn about these ethical expectations through training programs, coaching, reading manuals, company communications, and ethical codes, watching other employees and managers, and meeting with managers.

To make ethical codes work, a firm must have them written down and tailored to fit the industry that the firm is a part of. Codes must be communicated internally and externally, promoted, and updated regularly. Management from the top down must live the code and ensure that the code is enforced.

Bribery refers to the act of influencing others by giving them something. In Mexico, bribes are known as mordida; in Southeast Asia, kum-shaw; and in the Middle East, baksheesh. The Foreign Corrupt Practices Act of 1977 requires U.S. companies to account for and report international transactions accurately and prohibits bribes. The Act states that companies found guilty of paying bribes to foreign officials can be fined up to $1 million, and individual employees may be fined up to $10,000. While considered unethical in the United States, bribery is considered an unofficial part of doing business in many countries.

People Who Blow the Whistle

Whistleblowing generally involves an individual with unique knowledge of unethical actions, who uses public communication to let others know what is happening. A *whistleblower* can be someone who is an insider to the organization or someone who is an outsider to the firm such as suppliers, vendors, or professionals in the field. Whistleblowers have saved lives, prevented injuries and disease, and stopped corruption that would otherwise threaten the public. Whistleblowing is a personal act of conscientious, and the whistleblower often puts himself or herself at personal risk. Retaliation is not unusual, which is why most whistleblowers first try to rectify the problem internally before going public. Whistleblowers need credibility to deflect some of the retaliation and accusations that others may make against them.

Whistleblowing is part of our democratic value system that promotes free dissemination of information, which allows individuals to make informed decisions. Window into Practical Reality 4.4 illustrates whistleblowing by an outsider (Johnson et al. 2004).

Window into Practical Reality 4.4

External Whistleblower

A technician at MeritCare Health Systems in Fargo, North Dakota, first made the observation that women taking Fen-Phen had more valvular abnormalities than other women of the same age. When he discussed the findings with the interventional cardiologist at MeritCare, the cardiologist called Mayo to discuss the findings. The two cardiologists wrote an article for the *New England Journal of Medicine* and broke the story to the press. Armed with the published risks, users of the drug could make an informed decision as to whether to continue taking Fen-Phen. A month later American Home Products withdrew fenfluramine and dexfenfluramine from the market.

- What, if any, risk did the technician take in reporting the adverse data?
- What were the potential benefits of whistleblowing versus not blowing the whistle?

So, what influences a person to become a whistleblower? Whistleblowing happens when a member of an organization feels that the organization is not acting in an ethical way. An ethical dilemma exists in that the employee's ethical code and the firm's ethical code do not match. Generally, the whistleblower has a higher than average education, professional and social status, a group affiliation that encourages a whistleblowing mindset, and a culture with strong norms. Utilitarianism and strong moral beliefs compel the individual to tell authorities about the wrongdoings. The whistleblowing phenomenon has been increasing since the 1960s. Figure 4.2 illustrates the communicative act involved in whistleblowing.

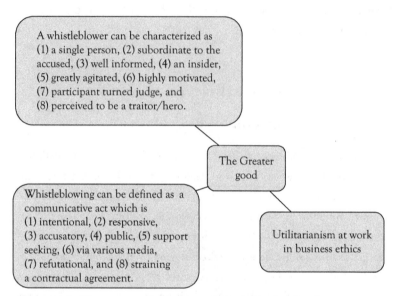

Figure 4.2 *The communicative act of whistleblowing for the greater good*

Whistleblowers often have a conflict between being loyal to the firm and doing what is best for the stakeholders of the firm. An employee may simply leave the firm and find another job; however, some choose to be a whistleblower while still employed by the firm. Culture influences the likelihood that whistleblowing will occur. For example, in Japan where people are more loyal to the firm and culturally are collectivistic, you will see less whistleblowing than in the United States, which is individualistic, and where employees are more transient between companies.

Other conflicts the whistleblower must deal with are his or her ethical obligations to the profession, family, livelihood, and colleagues, as well as obligation to the public and one's personal moral obligations. It is clear that whistleblowing is a utilitarian act with potentially severe consequences for the whistleblower. For this reason, whistleblowers often anonymously leak information to the media or regulatory authorities. For example, a whistleblower at WorldCom leaked e-mails to the press and federal officials, as described in the Window into Practical Reality 4.5.

Window into Practical Reality 4.5

How Leaks of E-mails Helped Worldcom Fall to Its Knees

Even though the company no longer exists, some WorldCom executives were imprisoned for lengthy sentences as a result of ethics violations.

David Meyers, a former WorldCom controller, tried to silence Steven Brabbs, a vice president for international finance, for questioning some accounting practices at WorldCom. The series of leaked e-mails that chronicled the ethical breach led to the downfall of the entire company. It is unclear who leaked the e-mails to the press and federal officials, yet, it is clear that the friction between Mr. Meyers and Mr. Brabbs was based on their entirely different values and personal ethics governing their conduct at work. On the one hand, Meyers could easily argue that his behavior was rooted in a sense of duty for WorldCom's very survival; nevertheless, Brabbs could argue the same thing. Yet, both men experienced totally different outcomes because of their moral position on reporting the financial information of the publicly traded company. Meyers's view on ethical conduct led to the downfall of the entire company. It appears the vast majority of the stakeholders in the WorldCom case believed that cooking the books is an immoral act (Feder 2002).

- If you were an accountant with WorldCom at the time, would you have blown the whistle by leaking the e-mails? Would it matter what you would do if you have three children dependent on you, and a mortgage payment due each month?
- Is there ever a time when leaking e-mails is a bad thing to do when a company is doing bad things?

Another example of a publicized whistleblower is Edward Snowden, who blew the whistle on the National Security Agency (NSA) spying on e-mails and phone calls. Had he stayed in the United States after blowing the whistle, he probably would be in jail. However, he chose to leave the country with sensitive data and is now considered a traitor by some. Others are thankful that he brought out the fact that the U.S. government was in fact gathering information without legal jurisdiction to do so from the courts. No matter which side you are on in this case, it illustrates the complexities that a whistleblower must consider before speaking out.

Ethical Guidelines

When considering guidelines for making ethical judgments, a person begins with his or her personal values and beliefs. If the individual has been a member of a society for an extended period of time, the values of the society, which are generally in the form of laws, will provide the second set of guidelines. If the organization has a written code of ethics, that will serve as the third set of guidelines to consider when making ethical decisions.

Problems happen when these sets of guidelines are in conflict or when different interpretations exist. For instance, what do you do if you are in another country and need to run electrical service to operate a manufacturing plant, but the local person wants a bribe to do so and the local culture says this is okay? The U.S. government says it is wrong to pay a bribe, but you know that if your company does not do so, it will be months before the plant will actually be running. Some firms have been known to hire a local consultant and let the consultant pay the bribe so that they are not directly knowledgeable about the situation. In your own country, what is right and wrong is much clearer than in another country where values and beliefs can be very different from your own. When you are in another country, you are caught in the dilemma of whether to follow their values, beliefs, and laws rather than your own which may be quite different.

Analyzing an ethical dilemma can be done by identifying the legal implications of the situation, finding and applying an appropriate code of ethics to the situation, implementing an ethical solution, and then

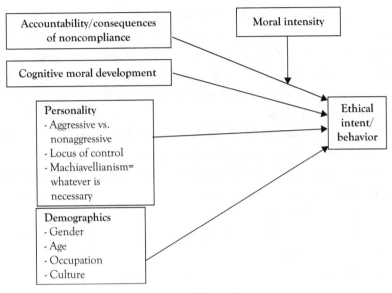

Figure 4.3 Ethical decision-making model

Source: Adapted from Beu, Buckley, and Harvey (2003, p. 90).

communicating that solution both internally and externally if necessary. The model shown in Figure 4.3 illustrates how people's ethical codes interact to determine behavior. Managers with *Machiavellian personalities* are people who believe manipulating others purely for political or personal gain is acceptable conduct in business. Therefore, the model shows that *Machiavellianism* refers to managers who are willing to do whatever is necessary to achieve their goals. These managers have no compunction in wrongdoing because they feel such behavior is perfectly acceptable.

According to Kohlberg, a leading moral development theorist, employees with higher levels of cognitive moral development will make ethical decisions more often than those with lower levels of cognitive moral development (Kohlberg 1969). Individuals with a propensity toward higher hostility and aggression will have more unethical intentions than individuals with lower hostility and aggression (Beu, Buckley, and Harvey 2003). *Locus of control* is the employee's sense of how much control he or she has over events or outcomes they can attain. When an employee desires to control the situation, he or she has an internal locus of control and will be less satisfied with a directive or dictatorial leader. These employees behave more ethically than employees with external locus of control, people who feel less control over events and need to be told what to do (Trevino and Youngblood 1990). Employees with high Machiavellianism tend to engage in more unethical behavior than those with a low score. Employee who live their religious faith will make moral choices based on their teleology.

Sometimes individuals' ethical values differ from those of their own culture, the company that employs them, or their managers' values. For example, a woman professional from the Middle East with an infant daughter might elect to immigrate to the United States because her home country prohibits women from voting, attending school, and driving cars. Many times, such ethical dilemmas stem from cultural meanings that the individual does not share with the macroculture. When this happens, the individual may choose to compartmentalize his or her life using the corporate ethics at work, but using his or her cultural ethics at home and in the corresponding cultural community. The person could adopt the values of the host culture or completely deny the host-culture values.

Research has shown that many employees believe that ethics is deteriorating due to worrying about the bottom line first, and with superiors who are only concerned with positive financial results. These expectations can lead employees to cut corners on quality control, cover up negative issues, misuse sick days, deceive customers, steal, and pressure others into inappropriate actions. Other actions that employees may consider which could benefit them personally include cheating on expense accounts, discriminating against coworkers, paying or accepting kickbacks, fixing prices, and other types of fraud. In business, as in many other actions in life, people are confronted with moral problems that their habitual responses cannot resolve easily, thus, they must reflect consciously on what they believe to be the right and wrong responses to such dilemmas.

While deliberate dishonesty hurts relationships, many times milder expressions of dishonesty will be forgiven. Telling your spouse of 40 years that he or she still looks as good as the day you got married may be good medicine for the marriage. Unfortunately, little white lies can become big problems and lead to major consequences. Managerial communications reflect ethical ideals within the firm. When managers create job descriptions and then use those job descriptions to evaluate employees, they are setting the requirements for the position. If they chose to deviate from the job description to assess performance, the employees will probably feel they have not been treated fairly.

Mission statements are constructed to let stakeholders know the firm's mission. If the mission is aligned with the values of the organization, it can be useful for guiding the behavior of management and employees. Mission statements are useless; however, when they are disregarded or not understood. How a manager describes organizational or departmental achievements is important. Is credit given to the person or team that made it happen, or does the manager take credit for the achievement? Taking credit for another's work should never happen, as a manager will get credit by giving credit to his or her worker's accomplishments. After all, the manager hired the people and coached them. Employees respond better to a manager who is concerned about them as individuals.

As important as sharing success, is the ability to accept responsibility for problems that develop and find solutions. For instance, when companies reduce employee benefits, the way the change is explained and how employees view the financial management of the firm have a lot to do with how well the changes are accepted. Marketing has the responsibility of selling what the firm offers, and public relations is charged with building goodwill for the organization and protecting its image. How marketing persuades customers through advertising has an ethical dimension. The classic phrase "let the buyer beware" came about because of organizations that were not always ethical in the way they chose to produce and sell their products. The term "if it is too good to be true, it probably is," is another way of saying "buyer beware." While many companies are responsible in their product offerings and sales tactics, some are not. Investors with Stanford Financial who were getting better returns on their investments than they could get anywhere else should have asked more questions. As it is, many lost all they had invested at Stanford. The Federal Bureau of Investigation reported in an article on its website, "Former Executives of Stanford Financial Group Entities Sentenced to 20 Years in Prison for Roles in Fraud Scheme." The report shows clearly the high costs of financial fraud, with one former executive receiving a sentence of 110 years in prison (U.S. Department of Justice 2013).

Strategic ambiguity exists when someone is purposefully vague to derive personal or organizational benefit. Not everyone believes that organizations should always have open communication. Those individuals would argue that strategically ambiguous communication is required in certain situations. However, strategic ambiguity complicates communication:

- It allows the source to both reveal and conceal, and to save face if necessary.
- It allows policy interpretation that could do more harm than good, and then the interpretations could be denied.
- Statements that are strategically ambiguous can mean different things at different points in time. (Eisenberg and Goodall 2001)

Unified diversity is giving different meanings to the same message. People will tend to interpret the message to fit their situation. While everyone would not interpret it the same, they would all embrace the message. For example, President Obama's campaign slogan for "Change" was interpreted differently among voters as the particular change that they wanted individually. Ambiguity can foster organizational change and creativity by leaving workers room to expand beyond direct commands. Preserving privilege and deniability happen when things go wrong and the people in authority claim that people did not understand what was said. This allows them to deny the workers' interpretation, protect their own position, and deny personal culpability (Eisenberg and Goodall 2001).

Summary

Business ethics has been in the forefront of business professionals' minds recently due to the number of unethical business situations that have become public. Personal ethics and the ethics of the culture are at times divergent, and ethical values vary considerably from one culture to the other. The current rift in American culture seems to be based on extreme positions of values and beliefs coming from both the far left and far right of the cultural spectrum. Five theories applicable to understanding ethical dilemmas faced by business people are consequentialism, decision theory, deontology, teleology, and utilitarianism.

Personal ethics are never exactly the same for all employees. Disagreements between secular values and religious values lead to conflicts of personal ethics and societal ethics that might not ever be resolved. Clearly stated organizational standards can help companies alleviate some of the bad ethical choices that employees could make. Training employees on the ethical standards of the organization and modeling ethical behavior from the top down are important elements of an ethical organization. Globalization involves consideration of different ethical perspectives. Unethical actions may be exposed by a whistleblower who is not able to get people inside the company to listen and change the problematic behavior.

CHAPTER 5

Conflict Resolution

Objectives

After reading this chapter, you will be able to:

1. differentiate psychological conflict from social conflict;
2. identify levels of organizational conflict;
3. describe different conflict management styles;
4. describe various methods of exerting psychological and social influence;
5. apply techniques to successfully negotiate, mediate, and arbitrate conflict.

Introduction

Conflict often happens when there are opposing options from which to select. Conflict is inevitable in business activity. The handling of conflict both inside and outside an organization depends on the personalities, history, and hierarchy of the firm. Lawyers and courts must at times become involved to settle conflicts that have gotten out of control simply because sufficient guidelines for resolving issues internally were not there. Precipitating events that were not handled effectively often lead to full-fledged conflicts. Courts are the last means of conflict resolution.

Conflict resolution depends on the predisposing elements and factors that exist within individuals and their communicative actions (intrapersonal, interpersonal, or group). Do the individuals involved anticipating a resolution that is win–win, win–lose, lose–lose, or lose–win? The attractiveness of options and the willingness of all parties to seek a mutually agreeable solution influence the type of communication that will be most effective in resolving the conflict.

Psychological and Social Conflict

A conflict that occurs within the individual is a *psychological conflict,* and the confronted person has options that are either attractive or unattractive. An *attractive conflict* is one in which the individual has a decision to make that has options he or she likes, while an *unattractive conflict* is one in which the individual does not have a desirable option. A conflict that occurs between individuals or groups is a *social conflict.* Social conflict can also be either attractive or unattractive, depending on the availability of desirable outcomes.

Conflict crosses the three of the five levels of managerial communication (MC) discussed in Chapter 2: intrapersonal, interpersonal, or group communications. For example, when a manager can hire only one candidate from among three ideal candidates (these are attractive options), that manager can resolve the conflict through intrapersonal dialog. That same manager might also resolve the problem by asking a colleague for input on the matter. If three managers are in charge of allocating limited funds for employee bonuses and the managers who are assigned the task disagree on allocating the funds, the conflict will likely be resolved in face-to-face meetings. *Personal conflicts* exist when two or more people in the group do not get along with one another. Some people enjoy keeping everything in turmoil, while others prefer a more calming and nurturing environment. In many cases, just changing one person in a group can entirely alter how the group gets along. When one person does not like someone else in the group, the ensuing conflict affects not only the two individuals but also the entire group.

Substantive conflicts involve individuals not agreeing with the others' analysis of issues. Substantive conflict may result in creative ways of solving problems as the opposing sides work through the substantive conflict issues.

Window into Practical Reality 5.1 provides an excerpt from an article published in *Supervision* explaining the challenges managers can face when they have a psychological conflict, whether the options are attractive or unattractive.

Window into Practical Reality 5.1

Challenges of Psychological Conflict

Psychological Conflict—when the Options are Intrapersonal

A psychological conflict is one where a manager has opposing options that he or she alone can resolve. When the decision is solely the manager's decision it is intrapersonal. *Intrapersonal* conflict is the reflective internal dialog a person has with himself or herself concerning the pros and cons of opposing options from which they must select. The options can be psychologically attractive (favorable to a lesser degree) or psychologically unattractive (unfavorable to a greater degree).

Psychologically Attractive Options

For example, a general manager of a busy upscale hamburger restaurant has posted a position to hire a shift supervisor from the existing staff. If the general manager has sole authority to make the hiring decision, then that manager has a psychological conflict. Reflective *internal dialog* occurs when the manager sincerely weighs the pros and cons of each option fairly. In the event that 3 ideal candidates are interviewed, say out of 20 qualified applicants, it is a good conflict to have. Nevertheless, it is at this point that the general manager can become the source of bad conflict.

When selecting the person for the supervisor position, the general manager might have a tendency to procrastinate. Perhaps the manager is concerned that the two other highly productive employees not selected might quit. The conflict becomes bad when the general manager engages in destructive internal dialog for a prolonged period, and the delay in the decision results in a climate of uncertainty. This is one example when the manager is guilty of over thinking the options for too long. A nondecision (or long-delayed decision) in most cases can be worse than a swift decision. It is better that the general manager explains to the two employees why they were not selected. They need to know that they are appreciated and what plans there are for them in the future, rather than allowing them to frame their own opinions about a long delay. Options are rarely the source for true conflict: managers' procrastinating important decisions are the source of bad conflict situations. The pressure intensifies even more when the psychological options are unattractive.

Psychologically Unattractive Options

Psychologically unattractive options are the opposite of attractive options. For example, if the aforementioned general manager has the sole authority to terminate the employment of 5 experienced employees out of 50 employees (a 10 percent reduction in staff), all of whom have scored very closely in annual evaluations, educational achievements, training, and experience, this decision can be very unattractive. People with high moral character do not enjoy being the cause for ending someone else's job.

The internal dialog can be vexing for the terminating manager. If the general manager has personal knowledge of the family or the unique circumstances of the employees subject to termination, choosing what to do can be perplexing. What if one of the employees slated for termination is a newly hired 25-year-old single mother of two, with one of her children being just 4 months old? For this reason, it is better to share unfavorable decision making with a team, whereby, weighing the unattractive options can be debated. At this point a final decision becomes a social conflict that can be resolved interpersonally.

Source: Bell (2013).

Procedural conflict happens when written strategies and policy statements actually keep a group from carrying out their responsibilities effectively. Over utilization of rules is an example of a procedural conflict that results in the hindrance of a group's ability to be creative or make changes. To avoid such a constraint, Apple made creativity the rule. Former CEO Steve Jobs once said when asked about the importance of market research, that it was useless because people did not know what new invention they wanted next. Jobs recognized the risk of following procedural expectations that resulted in the creation of me-too products, rather than completely new items that would revolutionize the market. Figure 5.1 illustrates examples of the two levels of conflict and the three levels of MC necessary to resolve them.

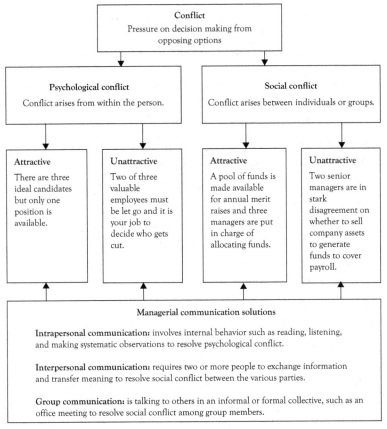

Figure 5.1 Levels of conflict and levels of managerial communication solutions

Managing Conflict

Conflict can be a good thing in some business situations. Out of conflict can come creativity, different values and perceptions, and new ways by which teams can be more productive. A phenomenon known as *groupthink,* or failure to think outside the box due to group pressure or expectations for conformity, can negatively affect group decision making when the group suppresses or punishes objective critical thinking. In some cases, unfettered groupthink can result in hysteria. Window into Practical Reality 5.2 is a summary of the hysteria that resulted from unfettered groupthink that occurred at Evergreen State College.

Window into Practical Reality 5.2

Groupthink at Evergreen State College

Evergreen State College located in Olympia, Washington, will likely forever be known for its *Day of Absence*. Students changed the annual ritual from black students not attending classes for a day to one where they now wanted all white people to leave campus for a day. A few white professors refused to participate, based on their asserting their constitutional rights. What transpired thereafter seems to read like a story.

Groups of furious students of mixed races took over the campus, swarmed classrooms and offices, and falsely imprisoned faculty, administrators, and even the president of the college. Video evidence shows that they shouted piercing chants at their captives: "Hey Hey, Ho Ho, these racist teachers have got to go!" Why were the students so angry? Their hysteria was likely caused at least in part by unfettered groupthink.

White professors Bret Weinstein and Heather Heying, who refused to leave the campus, settled their discrimination lawsuit for hundreds of thousands of dollars outside of court with Evergreen State College.

Bret Weinstein and Heather Heying initially filed a $3.85 million tort claim against Evergreen, alleging that the school failed to protect them. They later dropped the suit and, after months of trying to negotiate a return to their jobs, agreed to resign after reaching a $500,000 settlement. After legal fees, they say it's about two years' joint salary. (Herzog 2018)

The groupthink at Evergreen appears to stem from a notion that white privilege is based on an unfair economic advantage accrued to white people based on their ancestry. The assumption is that white privilege still exists because white people of today are inseparable from their racist, slave-owning past. The president of Evergreen appears to have allowed A Day of Absence at Evergreen to occur for many years because of his complicity as a privileged white man; the day served for many years as a form of retroactive remedy for the past evil deeds of white Americans. Whites are viewed as the primary beneficiaries of ill-gotten gains based on the blood and toil of slaves; therefore, white people should not be entitled to benefit from the spoils of slavery.

Students at Evergreen echoed the word *whiteness* because they believe in using emancipatory politics as collective punishment for wrongdoers. A Day of Absence to them was a reparation for their being members of an oppressed group. Apparently, the white students who acknowledged their wrongdoing and the wrongdoings of their forefathers were allowed to participate in the chants because black students perceived them as allies. Contrition served white students as a form of groupthink penance. Thus, all students believing in the hysteria could participate irrespective of color and could engage as full allies and join in on the call and answer routine: "Hey Hey, Ho Ho, these racist teachers have got to go!" Conformity was required absolutely. Professors and administrators at Evergreen who refused to go along with A Day of Absence were escorted to restrooms, harassed, demonized, and verbally abused.

- Were white faculty and administrators culpable for the oppression of black people just because they are white?
- How should the president of Evergreen have dealt with the groupthink hysteria to resolve the conflict?
- Is white privilege a real thing?
- Is black oppression a real thing?

Dialectic inquiry (a formal debate of opposing choices between members of the same group) and *devil's advocacy* (when one team member is assigned the task of criticizing and finding flaws in the team's choices) are good examples of constructive techniques used to avoid groupthink. Ideas that might otherwise never have been considered are often discussed because of conflict. Typically, managers will use rich channels, often referred to as *media richness*, of communication (face-to-face, videoconferencing) for ambiguous messages and less rich channels (e-mail, memos) for low-risk-oriented communications. A channel is richer when the receiver can understand the emotions behind the communication. The more cues that are available to the receiver, the more understanding there will be. Problems arise when managers do not realize the ambiguity of a situation, which often happens in intercultural business communication situations; or when a common language or language variation, is not shared by the group.

Many companies use internal jargon and numbers as a common language internally. The military and government organizations are known for having their own expressions and acronyms, but so do many public and private firms, clubs, and special interest groups.

Influence Strategies

Influence strategies are the methods used by an organization's personnel when using the power given to a particular position within the firm. These can be coercive or not coercive. When your boss is a dictator, you know that consideration of your ideas depends on whether they mirror his or her ideas. Employees tend to placate such bosses and to avoid offering solutions that do not fit the dictator's preferences. A boss whose mindset is inclusive of others' ideas will receive many more possible solutions to problems. Conflict is minimized and influence strategies are stronger in relationship dyads where there is trust and solidarity. The power structure and influence strategies used between two individuals are largely dependent upon the firm's overall use of influence strategies, the overall trust levels within the firm, and how influence strategies are reciprocated between dyads in the firm.

Our socialization creates automatic triggers for responding to others in various ways. These triggers serve as rules that govern our responses. For example, when someone gives you a gift and you did not think to give one in return, the compulsion you feel to hurry out and get a gift of equal value for that person can be overwhelming and is explained by the *reciprocity rule*. Some business people will use gift giving to gain an advantage in negotiations. Social programming tells us to assign a value to an item based on its cost. The *expensive equals good rule* applies when we assign a high value to an item because it was expensive. In reality, a $100 bottle of wine might not taste better than a $9 bottle.

The *commitment and consistency rule* teaches that once we start something, we should finish it. Logically speaking, abandoning some projects would be more sensible than seeing them through. Following the commitment and consistency rule has resulted in many disastrous management decisions and bankruptcies. For example, Coca Cola tried to improve its taste in the 1980s and ended up nearly destroying the brand, even though preliminary consumer data discouraged the change in formula. Ford went ahead with the release of the Ford Pinto against warnings from safety engineers, and cost itself millions of dollars in legal settlements and massive advertisement campaigns to assuage the public's distrust of its manufacturing capabilities. Managers, both nationally and internationally, must be on guard against using these "weapons of influence" when resolving conflicts. However, knowing how to use compliance psychology as a tool to influence positive behavior can strengthen your conflict resolution skills.

Conflict Management Styles

Conflict management styles can be categorized as avoidance, distributive, and integrative. *Avoidance style* involves minimizing or ignoring the conflict situation (Sillars et al. 1982) and is unassertive and uncooperative. *Distributive management style* is confrontational and generally one-sided, with one side conceding to the other (Putnam and Wilson 1982). Window into Practical Reality 5.3 provides an illustration of distributive management style at work.

Window into Practical Reality 5.3

Distributive Conflict

Sean was a director who felt that ordering people around would make them respond. He also did not feel it was necessary for him to explain his actions to his subordinates. If he did not like someone, he would arrange that person's work hours to be exactly what the individual did not want. When employees complained, they did not get a satisfactory answer. If the employee asked for a specific vacation time, the time was never available, again without any explanation. Employees also discovered that their work was never good enough. Sean would set objectives, but when the objectives were met, he made the workers redo the work according to new rules not given at the beginning. Managers like Sean change their minds and expect others to be able to read their minds and know what they want, and they enjoy treating subordinates as outsiders. Such people tend to have no real friends because they do not develop lasting relationships, and people may be scared of them. Frequently employees do not like bosses like Sean and often will leave or transfer away from the "Seans" of the world.

- What are some reasons that the "Seans" of the work world are allowed to become and remain as supervisors?
- What are some other unpopular supervisor behaviors that "turn off" subordinates?

Integrative style managers employ cooperative behaviors for a shared solution (Walton and McKersie 1965). How group conflict management norms evolve is particular to the members of the group and not easily predictable (Kuhn 1998). The management style of the person in charge is very important to what a group can achieve.

Kuhn and Poole (2000) found that over time groups tend to repeatedly use the same conflict management style for their decision making. They also found a significant relationship between conflict style and decision-making effectiveness, with integrative groups rated as highly effective and avoidance and distributive style groups as less so. Teams that manage conflict productively are also better facilitators and observers. Even when a topic was contentious and required a great deal of discussion, the integrative groups spent the time necessary to solve the disagreement. Conflict management involves both task and maintenance functions in the groups, with *task functions* including the completion of the assignment, and *maintenance functions* including taking care of the group members needs so that they work together effectively. The Window into Practical Reality 5.4 illustrates how a large company prepares its leadership to achieve conflict resolution.

Window into Practical Reality 5.4

FedEx Prepares Leaders for Conflict Resolution

FedEx is an example of an organization that strives to improve the conflict resolution skills of its managers through management communication training, media training, public speaking coaching, awards,
the inclusion of communication as a component of performance appraisals, and performance of an annual communication audit of the
corporation. What other examples of companies can you recall that
illustrate preparation for conflict resolution?

Another interesting study looked at departments in colleges and the
management models that were followed. In the *bureaucratic model,* conflict
happens but can be managed with clarifying roles and procedures. In the
political model, conflict is viewed as inevitable and normal. While in the
collegial model, conflict is perceived as abnormal and in need of elimina-
tion. The *anarchical model* is often seen when resources become scarce and
management has to make difficult decisions, which leads to widespread
conflicts. The type and degree of conflict tended to determine the management style applied, and most of the department chairs did not consistently
follow a single conflict management style (Stanley and Algert 2007).

Organizations generally develop acceptable conflict management
styles. However, the appointment of new managers can result in change
in the conflict management styles used. In recent years, we have seen a
number of CEOs appointed to "clean house." For instance, Jack Welch,
CEO at General Electric, fired the bottom 10 percent of managers every
year based on their performance appraisals. Over the long term, you may
ask whether this is the correct management style, considering where the
corporation is today.

Cultural Elements in Conflict

Cultural distance can affect which channels are acceptable to use between
a receiver and a sender. Managers of global operations quickly learn that
the channels that work at home often do not work abroad due to the

cultural distance between the dyads. Differences in personal constructs of belief systems and attitudes require the acceptance of a global mindset. One definition of a global mindset is

> ...the ability to develop and interpret criteria for personal and business performance that are independent from the assumptions of a single country, culture, or context: and to implement those criteria appropriately in different countries, cultures, and contexts. (Maznevski and Lane 2004, p. 4)

Accomplishing this global mindset is often easier said than done because gaps in technology, business strategy, and economics compound the challenge. Elements that affect cultural distance include language, geographical distance, differences in religion, and social structure. Training both employees and managers who will work well interculturally has been very successful in many organizations. Learning what is different between cultures, then watching out for those trouble spots, gives a global manager an advantage over the untrained manager.

A number of factors affect global communication strategies. For instance, a *cosmopolitan orientation* refers to that managers' concern with issues and events in the world. *Cognitive world orientation* is the ability to differentiate between environmental events and elements that exist in various cultures. *Cultural intelligence* is an aptitude for understanding and dealing with cultural differences. *Universalists* tend to see the impact of an event beyond their own culture, versus *particularists* who tend to look only at how an event affects their own group. Even when managers possess global understanding, having supportive networks is imperative to being successful internationally.

Effective conflict management and organizational decision making are needed to deal with individuals and groups in conflict. An organization's history and hierarchy also control the handling of conflict both inside and outside the organization. The communication pattern in conflict environments is often aggressive, which leads to the breakdown in the relationship. The voice, tone, word choice, and directness of the communication can also lead to conflict. When aggression, incivility, or competing interests have thwarted agreement and have created conflicts among individuals and groups that seem too difficult to resolve, then common goals and interest are essential. Humor, for example, can be an effective tool to reduce tension and enhance communication when applied with discretion during negotiation, mediation, or arbitration. Humor works best when everyone in the group is from the same culture, as what is perceived as humorous in one culture is not necessarily humorous in another culture. Many times, humor involves a play on words which does not translate well.

Laws and administrative principles often govern conflict resolution. Figure 5.2 illustrates the four main categories for adjudicating complex organizational issues that require conflict resolution: laws and organizational rules, negotiation, mediation, and arbitration.

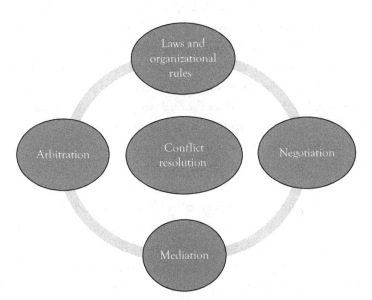

Figure 5.2 Conflict resolution governed by laws and organizational rules, negotiation, mediation, and arbitration

Under the illustrated categories, the rules for resolving conflicts are more formulaic, and the adjudication process will involve a disinterested (unbiased) third party such as a judge, mediator, or arbitrator. Some situations require going through all four types of conflict resolution, and others will only require one of the conflict resolution methods.

Laws and Organizational Rules

Laws are written by a government or the judicial system. What you write and say in conjunction with your job duties can have legal implications both for you personally as well as for the corporation. For example, it is important to realize that even deleted e-mails are traceable, and recorded phone conversations are the norm in many organizations.

In addition to laws that apply, firms often have guidelines on how to write or discuss hiring or firing decisions, claims, contracts, labor negotiations, pricing policies, reference letters, sales letters, warranties, or other information. Company rules may exist for communicating via e-mail and the phone and for using the Internet. For example, some employers have tried to restrict employee use of technology and the computer to business usage only, which in some cases has resulted in employees taking the employer to court.

Arbitrators and courts have upheld employer rules in many cases, relying on *stare decisis,* the Latin phrase meaning to stand by an earlier decision that creates a precedent. Webster defines *stare decisis* as "a doctrine or policy of following rules or principles laid down in previous judicial decisions unless they contravene the ordinary principles of justice." As an example, viewing pornography at work is widely recognized as reason for termination, as there are a number of cases in different states on this issue. Sending sexually harassing e-mail messages is also reason for dismissal. On the other hand, the rights of workers to forward chain e-mails has been upheld; only when employees had been told prior to the offense that the practice was against company policy could they be fired. Hate language is also not permissible in most offices (Lichtash 2004).

The permanence of e-mail chains often wreak havoc on careers. Window into Practical Reality 5.5 illustrates a recent example of the dangers of e-mail.

Communications are considered as owned by the company when they are generated using the company's computer and e-mail systems. Court cases have established that when a company has notified their employees that systems are being monitored and employees have given their consent, the company can legally use surveillance to monitor the use of such equipment. It is also acceptable for an employer to use a firewall to filter out websites that they deem unacceptable and to block sites that reduce productivity.

Window into Practical Reality 5.5

The Bridgegate Scandal Uncovered via E-mail Communications

Governor Chris Christie of New Jersey found himself under investigation because of a leaked e-mail written by his former Deputy Chief of Staff, Bridget Anne Kelly. The e-mail stated, "It's time for some traffic jams." Her e-mail was sent to dozens of recipients, which linked other staffers directly to what became known as "Bridgegate." Staffers in the Christie administration allegedly caused days of traffic jams on the George Washington Bridge—the busiest bridge in the world—as political retribution against a sitting mayor of a small New Jersey town who had not endorsed Christie's reelection. Christy's staff ordered the bridge closed on Monday, September 9, 2013. It is illegal for employees of the State of New Jersey to use state resources for personal or political gain. Many careers stood on the verge of being ruined by the Bridgegate scandal. What communication lessons can be learned from the scandal?

Negotiation

Negotiation is a process of give and take to resolve a conflict. Managers negotiate with upper management, subordinates, and other managers for sharing scarce resources, motivating workers to do more, getting more time to finish projects, and working out problems with other corporate departments. If a manager is not successful at negotiating, their department's productivity can be compromised, as well as the organization's overall. Failed negotiations can demoralize workers and create a hostile work situation. The ability to network is an essential skill, when a manager needs to negotiate a solution to a given situation. New managers can assist in developing networks through mentoring. A mentor helps the mentee learn the ropes of the business and become familiar with who has the power to help achieve goals. When you negotiate as a manager, you must balance what is good for the corporation with what is good for your workers and yourself. If management assigns you additional work, you as the manager may need to negotiate if your unit can do the work effectively or not, if it will require overtime, if you will need to add additional personnel, or if you need additional funds.

When managers do not choose to negotiate with others in the firm, they make a choice to avoid the situation, comply with the situation, or co-opt and try to control the situation. While avoiding a situation may work for little problems, it generally allows major situations to worsen. *Complying* with the situation implies that the manager feels that the situation is not major and not worth the effort involved in changing the mindset of others. Attempts to *co-opt and control* the situation result when the manager feels he or she knows the best solution and wants others to acquiesce.

When choosing to negotiate, the manager may merely communicate information, or attempt to engage the other side in a conversation. Once a manager decides what the outcomes should be, there is a tendency to communicate the information to the other party, rather than engaging people in a conversation and selling the idea. Smythe (2007) found that engaging employees increased company focus, performance, staff retention, morale, and profitability. Opening up decision making to include as many employees as is feasible in the process, as opposed to using a top–down model of decision making, can be very profitable for a firm. While the best negotiation model is a win–win strategy, sometimes that is not possible. Managers are continually negotiating salaries, budget increases or decreases, office space, technology usage, and various other operating funds. There may be limits to what they can offer or what they can pay for materials and maintain a positive bottom line. Window into Practical Reality 5.6 provides an example of negotiations at work.

Many negotiation errors are due to unthinking, rude, symbolic, and nonverbal cues associated with the behaviors of one or both of the parties involved in the negotiation. Table 5.1 illustrates commonly made errors during negotiation (Cellich 1997). These behaviors can have really costly consequences, as illustrated in Table 5.1.

Effective negotiators avoid these common mistakes, emphasize areas of agreement, and consider the long-term consequences of their decisions. Before going into a negotiation situation, it is important for managers to have a plan prepared from the facts as they know them, and then be willing to change their stance as new information surfaces. Conflict naturally

Window into Practical Reality 5.6

General Motors and Production in China

The AFL-CIO has been a very strong union, with a long-standing reputation of having the members' interest at heart. When General Motors (GM) asked for concessions in the labor contract and the union did not budge, GM started planning for a future without the union. By building and selling cars in China, GM management did not have to deal with the union, and the union could not control or unionize the Chinese workers. GM saw the China solution as ideal; Chinese workers were willing to work for less pay, and car sales were growing with the rise of a new Chinese middle class. GM could make more money for its stockholders by producing in China rather than in the United States.

In February 2012, GM announced that it was adding a third line to the Flint, Michigan plant; however, at the same time it announced plans to build a $1.7 billion plant in China that would produce 300,000 cars a year.

- Why did GM make these decisions?
- Why was the company willing to take so many jobs overseas?
- What are the unions missing?
- What part did the number of cars GM is selling in China play in these negotiations?
- Why did the union go for a win-lose strategy in the first place?
- Why did the union end up with a lose-win strategy?

includes a certain amount of ambiguity, adaptability, and apprehension. The ability to handle conflict successfully is the difference between a good leader and a placeholder.

Mediation

Mediators provide an unbiased and ethical point of view between two differing opinions. These individuals listen to both sides, while showing

Table 5.1 Negotiation errors and the interpretable consequences

Interpretable consequences

Negotiation errors	Unthinking	Rude	Symbolic	Nonverbal
Making a negative initial impression				X
Failing to listen and talking too much		X		
Assuming understanding by the other culture			X	
Failing to ask important questions	X			
Showing discomfort with silence			X	
Using unfamiliar and slang words	X	X		
Interrupting the speaker		X		
Failing to read the nonverbal cues	X		X	
Failing to note key points	X			X
Making statements that are irritating or contradictory		X	X	
Failing to prepare a list of questions for discussion	X			X
Being easily distracted			X	
Failing to start with conditional offers	X			
Failing to summarize and restate to ensure understanding	X		X	
Hearing only what they want to hear	X		X	
Failing to use first-class supporting materials	X		X	

compassion, providing impartial leadership, and guiding the parties to a solution. They help develop a solution that everyone can agree upon. Unless they develop a solution viewed as successful by all parties, the problem will return. A mediator's job is more than settling the case or problem; it is satisfying the parties that they have a fair decision. In successful mediation, both parties feel that the mediator is fair, respectful, and sensitive during the process.

Personality traits such as extraversion and agreeableness may be the bases of a mediator's success. *Extraversion* means that the person is talkative, sociable, and enjoys people. *Agreeableness* is the mediator's ability to be altruistic and cooperative. A mediator who is positive will find the participants to be more agreeable than one who is negative.

Teams within an organization base mediation on their identity within the organization and trust of their peers. When team members identify with the team, they are part of the "in-group" and view themselves positively. The team members will also be motivated to protect their group. If any members are not part of the in-group, then they are part of the "out-group," which reduces the performance of the team (Han and Harms 2010).

Social conflict can be categorized as either relationship conflict or task conflict. *Relationship* conflict being the conflict among the individuals of the group and *task* conflict refers to the disagreement over the solution of an issue. While relationship conflict can reduce or negate a team's ability to solve a task, a task conflict can actually lead to a better solution if properly mediated. The more transparent communication is, the less likelihood there will be for task or relationship conflict.

Han and Harms (2010) found that trust mediated the relationship between team identification and team conflict. When trust is broken, mediation is needed. While professional mediators can be called in, managers often act as mediators. In the mediating role, the manager listens to both parties' stories, shows interest in all sides, provides leadership to the situation, immediately deescalates the conflict, assures everyone of a fair process, guides the parties as necessary, assists the parties with their decisions pertaining to the situation, acts as a clearing house for information, discusses offers and counteroffers with the parties, is a reality check for all involved, and helps to reestablish an equilibrium (Noll 2009). The role of a mediator is important because if either or both parties feel slighted in anyway, the matter could go to court. The manager acting as mediator cannot appear threatening to the parties in any way. Much of what a mediator does is to help the people involved to control their emotions, discuss what has happened, and determine what needs to happen to correct the situation. Communication skills are paramount in a mediation session, and addressing the situation as soon as possible is always important rather than thinking it will go away.

Mediators who are part of the firm must also live with the decisions reached. If the problem is not truly resolved, the manager will be mediating again on the same problem. After completing the mediation, the manager should follow-up to see that the parties are in fact satisfied with the decisions. The greater the trust and the higher the quality of information that is shared, the more likely the parties will have a lasting resolution to their problems.

Arbitration

Arbitration is done by an outside person who is hired to resolve the situation; the arbitrator's decision is binding on both parties. The arbitrator decides how the conflict arbitration will proceed. An arbitrator will (1) issue a comprehensive scheduling order which will have all of the deadlines for both sides; (2) set down the claims, damages, counterclaims, and defenses; and (3) establish discovery time limits (Chambers 2009).

Arbitration is normally the last chance to find a solution to a problem without legal action. However, arbitration does not always prevent a matter from going to court. In general, an arbitration case is resolved in 8 months, while a court case may go on for 2 years. Employees generally fare better with arbitrators than with the courts in terms of settlements. Arbitration offers numerous advantages over litigation in court. With arbitration, the two sides have more control over the process than they do with litigation. Arbitration generally does not cost as much, is more flexible, gives the sides choices, provides a more level playing field for both sides, and allows each side some self-determination. The main difference between arbitration and litigation is who makes the decision. During litigation, trial attorneys decide where to file, and a judge is automatically assigned. During arbitration the sides decide on the number of arbitrators and their qualifications. Arbitrators follow the rules of the Federal Arbitration Act, and arbitration is more confidential than transactions in courts of law which tend to be public. While in court you can be held in contempt for failure to appear, that is not so in arbitration though you still must present your burden of proof just as in court. There is less paperwork involved with arbitration than with litigation.

Steps to Successful Conflict Resolution

Conflict resolution involves a number of steps, as illustrated in Table 5.2. The process of observing, analyzing, and evaluating must be completed for each step shown in Table 5.2. Following the steps will help you assure a win–win solution to the conflict. While resolving conflict requires a significant investment of time and energy, the resources are well spent when a satisfactory solution is reached.

Table 5.2 Eight steps to a successful resolution process

Step 1	Select a suitable location for the negotiations. A neutral site is usually the best location.
Step 2	Identify the agenda or policy issues in the negotiation, including the selection of negotiators, the role of individual aspirations, concern with protocol, and significance of the type of issue.
Step 3	Prepare the preliminary statement and limitation considerations. Determine a means to communicate clearly, including the nature of persuasive argument, value of time, and appreciation of cultural differences, anticipation of their moves, and areas for mutual understanding.
Step 4	Determine areas for deliberation, potential solutions of some issues, and issues with no apparent agreement. Establish bases of trust, recognize risk-taking propensity, internal decision-making systems, and techniques for persuasion.
Step 5	Narrow down differences to achieve consensus, emphasize commonalities of interest, and systematically search for alternatives. Understand limitations of your counterparts and use empathy and conflict management.
Step 6	Direct final negotiations and facilitate give and take necessary in the bargaining process. Strive for a win–win outcome.
Step 7	Contract or confirm the agreement. Consider the requirements of the countries involved in the dispute resolution and the expectations for agreements and written documents.
Step 8	Implement the agreement. For negotiations to be successful, the negotiators must become adept through continual observation, analysis and evaluation, at catching the problems, and adapting negotiation strategy.

Source: Casse and Deol (1991).

Summary

Conflicts result when opposing options confront an individual. Conflict can occur on two levels: the psychological and the social. Psychological conflict occurs within the individual, and social conflict occurs between individuals or groups. Hysteria can occur when groupthink is unfettered, leading to an out-of-control organization and costly tort lawsuits against the organization. The two best methods to avoid groupthink are devil's advocacy and dialectic inquiry. The three levels of MC required to resolve conflict are intrapersonal communication, interpersonal communication, and group communication.

Successful management of conflict within a firm is dependent upon the skills of its leaders. Conflict is not always negative, since creative ideas can emerge from it. When management uses richer channels of communication, employees are more likely to understand what they need to do. Responses to conflict can include things about conflict which can include avoidance, distributive, or integrative styles of communication, and the use of these styles tends to be related to the degree of formality of the organization.

Socialization creates automatic triggers for how we respond to others. These triggers are based on rules that govern our responses, including the *reciprocity rule,* the *expensive equal good rule,* and the *commitment and consistency rule.* Managing conflict is greatly influenced by cultural differences. Managing people with various cultural orientations requires a universalist view.

Managers are often called upon to act as mediators for internal problems. In arbitration, someone from outside of the firm conducts the process, and the arbitrator's decision is binding on all the parties.

Laws, negotiation, mediation, and arbitration aid in providing a backdrop of trust necessary for solving conflicts in the workplace. Managers, as well as the parties involved, have to live with the decisions reached. If the problem is not truly resolved, the manager will continue to have to work on the problem in the future. Training managers in conflict resolution is a worthwhile investment for firms.

CHAPTER 6

Communication Technology

Objectives

After reading this chapter, you will be able to:

1. define communication technology;
2. identify the proper and improper uses of communication technology in business;
3. describe three guidelines for conducting business meetings;
4. describe ways for conducting multicultural and virtual business meetings.

Introduction

Communication technology can be defined as any electronic system used by business people, not physically present in the same location, to exchange ideas or conduct business. The use of communication technology in today's society is viewed by many as excessive. Electronic devices appear as appendages to many people, and technology-assisted communication invades virtually every environment, including dinners, meetings, and even religious services. People often lose their sense of what is safe while using mobile devices when driving. Thousands of vehicular accidents are reported each year involving people texting while driving. People engrossed in text messages and other handheld communication functions while operating motor vehicles have caused a significant number of injuries and fatalities, to themselves as well as others. Texting while driving poses a terrible hazard to public safety, and the U.S. Department of Transportation has recently suggested that all cell phone use by drivers be banned. Some companies, such as Dupont, have safety directives that do not allow their employees to use mobile devices while driving company vehicles.

Some companies will fire individuals who have accidents while driving and using their cell phones for any purpose whatsoever.

The problems associated with drivers using cell phones is so dangerous that many jurisdictions have adopted significant restrictions on their use:

> Sixteen states, D.C., Puerto Rico, Guam, and the U.S. Virgin Islands prohibit all drivers from using handheld cell phones while driving. All are primary enforcement laws—an officer may cite a driver for using a handheld cell phone without any other traffic offense taking place. No state bans all cell phone use for all drivers, but 38 states and D.C. ban all cell phone use by novice drivers, and 20 states and D.C. prohibit it for school bus drivers . . . Washington was the first state to pass a texting ban in 2007. Currently, 47 states, D.C., Puerto Rico, Guam and the U.S. Virgin Islands ban text messaging for all drivers. (GHSA 2018, para 1)

In addition to safety issues while driving, data safety is also a serious challenge as massive amounts of critical data are carried from place to place on devices that can be easily stolen or hacked.

There are other important elements as well. In this chapter, we will discuss how communication technology in business settings enables modern managers to be more efficient and effective, which includes (1) proper uses of communication technology, (2) improper uses of communication technology, and (3) conducting multicultural and virtual business meetings.

Uses of Communication Technology

Communication technology affords many beneficial opportunities for communication in organizations but also poses various possibilities for exploitation and abuse.

Beneficial Uses of Communication Technology

Social media website such as Facebook and Twitter are popular among the millennial generation, and more and more baby boomers are also signing up to connect with friends and family. Companies also use social media communications to market their ideas and products. Software applications that utilize Voice-over-Internet-Protocol (VoIP) allow users to make voice calls over the Internet. When using a webcam-enabled device, users can see and talk in real time to individuals with similarly equipped hardware and software. Two common applications used for this purpose are Skype and Apple's FaceTime. Professionals use LinkedIn to stay in contact with friends and business associates. Instagram and Pinterest allow for photo sharing. YouTube is used widely by individuals, businesses, educational institutions, and government agencies to share video content. Any individual with a cell phone can live stream current events to the Internet in real time. In addition to enabling individuals to become overnight celebrities, live streaming enables businesses to reach the public with marketing information, testimonials of products, and messages from the CEO. Many businesses encourage their top executives to use Twitter for advertising purposes.

Individuals like their smartphones and communication devices, including the 44th president of the United States, Barack Obama. When newly elected president, Barack Obama, insisted on keeping his Blackberry, the Secret Service immediately went into action to find solutions to keep the president's e-mail communications private. While Obama loved his Blackberry, Trump loves to use Twitter.

Since his election in 2016, President Trump has used Twitter effectively to fend off attacks from the main stream media (MSM) which he has deemed fake news. Although President Trump did not invent the phrase "fake news," he certainly popularized it. A list of fake news sites developed by Melissa Zimdar, an assistant professor of communication at Merrimack College went viral in November 2016 (Bailey and Becker 2016). The list was intended to identify and expose fake news sites, in an attempt to help ordinary citizens sort through the thicket of information on the Internet (Zimdar 2016). However, her list was quickly used by CNN as a means of discrediting voices advocating for the president. Trump then turned the rhetoric against CNN and the MSM and has used the notion of "fake news" successfully ever since then. He now routinely antagonizes and baits these outlets in his rallies and Twitter posts with what he is now calling "very fake news" (Wallace 2016). His cunning use of Facebook and his indefatigable Twitter attacks are viewed as important elements in his defeat of Hillary Clinton for the presidency (Lapowsky 2016).

Smartphones are very useful for individuals and business because people can send and receive complete e-mails, including downloads of attachments with excellent screen resolution. Thousands of phone apps are available that allow users to perform a varied assortment of work tasks, enjoy a host of leisure activities, and engage in a myriad of consumer activities. For instance, the popular barcode reader apps for real-time price comparison shopping facilitate purchase decisions. Stores such as Sears with price guarantees find that thrifty shoppers utilize their smartphones to demand the lowest price or go elsewhere to shop for bargains.

Employees as well as private citizens use corporate blogs to find out what is happening in companies. Companies can utilize blogs for sharing information with employees before making the information available to the public on the Internet or through other media sources. Jamming involves using an internal website to educate employees and create a positive company culture. Window into Practical Reality 6.1 discusses this current use of technology by one organization.

Window into Practical Reality 6.1

Jamming at IBM

IBM started jamming in the late 1990s by using their corporate intranet to engage employees in a live companywide conversation. The idea behind the technology is to get ideas and develop new possibilities, and participants can enter and add to a jam at any time. On one occasion, the company used jamming to develop a set of work values. For 72 hours, 50,000 IBMers followed the jam, and 10,000 posted comments. IBM found that their employees participated more in this informal jamming mechanism than they did in formal meetings, perhaps because of perceived anonymity and the view that everyone's voice was equal (Birkinshaw and Crainer 2007).

The Internet has revolutionized the job search process. For job seekers, corporate websites provide listings of available positions, along with the means to submit applications online. Resumes can often be submitted online by simply cutting and pasting into the format provided. The website also provides an easy way to find out about a company before an interview. The job of hiring agents is also simplified by having access to resumes that are arranged in the same format. Word searches can be used to identify candidates whose qualifications provide the closest match to job requirements. LinkedIn provides a convenient way for job seekers to share their credentials and also to be discovered by companies looking for potential hires who possess a specific skill set.

Smartphones do much more than provide users with the ability to make and receive phone calls. An expanding assortment of features enables users to communicate in multiple ways. Researchers have found that demographic characteristics, such as gender, age, or residence (rural or urban community), can be used to predict their usage of some phone features. For instance, female college students tend to use the e-mail feature significantly more than the game features. Tween and teenage users of communication technology devices are now the focus of targeted marketing from apparel retailers, who realize this age group cannot be reached through the more traditional media outlets (Stark et al. 2008). Victoria's Secret's PINK brand was developed and launched specifically for the tween demographic, and its marketing campaigns targeting this age group integrate electronic social networking to reach tweens with product offerings (Bell et al. 2011).

Managers must make an effort to keep up with new technology and learn how to use it properly in business settings. Obviously, the younger the employees, the more in tune they will likely be with new technologies. Some examples of popular communication technology applications and their uses for business are shown in Table 6.1.

A firm's ability to react quickly in providing current information to customers can be crucial to its image and reputation. For example, an insurance company can make use of social media after a natural disaster to provide policy holders with current claim contact phone numbers in the event the client has experienced a loss.

Companies can also interface more effectively with their internal constituents because of web 2.0 technologies that make it easy to develop wikis, blogs, podcasts, and online training programs. Younger generations tend to go to these sources for information more frequently than they do to newspapers, magazines, or news programs.

Table 6.1   Business applications of communication technology

Communication technology	Associated brands	Business applications
Social networking sites	Facebook, Instagram, Pinterest, and Craigslist; and for dating: OkCupid, PlentyOfFish, Match.com, and Tinder	Public awareness, broad audience, mass marketing or market segmentation, banner ads and commercials, streaming video, and employment vetting process
Person-to-person	Smartphones and mobile devices (Sony, Motorola, iPhone, Blackberry, Droid, Tablets)	Text messaging, bill payments, billing receipts, e-mail, file downloads, attachments, alerts, and barcode readers for comparison shopping
Search engines	Google, Bing, and Yahoo	Access to billions of pages of information, government documents, and legacy systems can be integrated with search engine protocols, e.g., online banking
Blogging	Twitter, web-based blogs	Brand awareness, real-time information direct to fans, or business associates
VoIP	Skype, Wimba, duo, FaceTime	Conferencing, video, audio, and long-distance virtual meetings
eReaders	iPad, NOOK, and Kindle Fire	e-Book downloads, extensive business e-Book library in electronic files

Improper Uses of Communication Technology

Companies recognize the benefits of communication technologies for collaboration, communication, and networking. However, while recognizing the enormous potential for customer development externally and employee communication internally, they have legitimate concerns about risks to proprietary information, privacy, and security. One law that affords protection to electronic communication in the United States is the *Electronic Communications Privacy Act* (ECPA). The ECPA extended the provisions of the Federal Wiretap Act of 1968, which addressed interception of conversations using "hard" telephone lines, but this did not apply to interception of computer and other digital and electronic communications (U.S. Department of Justice, Office of Justice Programs 2013). The current law dictates that employers must notify their employees when

Internet usage is monitored. Once notified, employees who use the system have given their implied consent to the monitoring.

Using technology to steal information is relatively easy. Cyber stalkers and other Internet criminals are not limited to one geographic location. Hacking can occur in a wide variety of ways. Credit card information can be stolen when people swipe their cards at the point of sale, personal and financial information can be hacked from computers or mobile devices when using unsecured Internet connections or when lacking updated security software, and sensitive information can be intercepted by viewing or listening to communications over wireless networks. Individuals must be aware that their devices are susceptible to hacking and ensure that adequate measures are taken to secure their data.

Some abuses of technology are not necessarily illegal, yet they pose serious ethical questions. An example of risky behavior involving technology is the practice of sexting (people forwarding nude photos of themselves to friends or complete strangers they find online). These photos can be repeatedly forwarded and also land on pornographic websites. A number of politicians and celebrities have suffered embarrassment and loss of status after being exposed through sexting. Another communication practice of ethical concern is cyber bullying—the use of electronic devices to convey messages of hate, hostility, and violence.

Cyber bullying at work can also occur when people use technology to say things that should be discussed in a face-to-face setting but instead are done online behind someone's back. A person can be bullied at work by a supervisor, who makes inappropriate comments (e.g., memorializing disparaging comments in a permanent record). Sometimes participating in a company debate by responding to an internal request for feedback on a controversial topic can backfire on the respondent, as is the case with James Damore, former Google engineer. Damore was fired for harassment for comments he sent in a memo. Damore wrote a manifesto on women's "choices" attempting to explain why women are underrepresented in science, technology, engineering and math (STEM) subjects. When his leaked internal 10-page memo went viral, Damore was fired from Google. Damore is now suing Google for discrimination against him based on his race, gender, and rights to free speech; his class action lawsuit, now joined by others, apparently has legal standing and is slowly making its way through the hierarchy of the courts (Guynn 2018). Communication technology misuse can have long-lasting negative effects on victims. The courts will determine if Damore's attempt to participate in a controversial Google-driven debate on the lack of women in STEM was an exercise in his free speech, and if his termination from Google was wrongful; conversely, the courts might side with Google that Damore exemplified hate speech and bullying in his memo that went viral.

Texting has become quite popular with business for both internal and external communication purposes. A whole abbreviation language has emerged, for instance OOO (out of office), FYI (for your information), and EOD or EOB (end of day or business). While texting is useful for quick exchange of information, business activity often necessitates a more formal record of communication for verification and historical reference. The use of texting has become very popular among businesses. In addition, phone companies do have permanent records of text messages, which can be subpoenaed for legal purposes (Burke 2015). Other forms of written communication such as e-mail provide such a record, and phone conversations are easily recorded for historical purposes. Correct grammar and spelling and careful use of abbreviations is important in texting for business, as it conveys an appropriate tone and helps the receiver decode your message properly.

Abuses of technology take many forms, such as getting into e-mail or texting arguments or using technology to layoff or fire employees rather than confront them face-to-face. It's not generally a good idea for employees to tweet or make negative comments on their Facebook page about a manager or the company. While the company may not like such communication, courts have ruled in favor of the employee in several cases as illustrated in Window into Practical Reality 6.2.

Another example of communication technology abuse is the sharing of classified and confidential information with unauthorized parties. A recent incident at the Pentagon posed a threat to U.S. national security when Bradley Manning, a 22-year-old soldier, leaked nearly 750,000 military files and classified U.S. intelligence reports to an internationally based public protest website called WikiLeaks. Manning confessed and pleaded guilty to dozens of charges. Manning was subsequently

Window into Practical Reality 6.2

A Woman Is Illegally Fired for Remarks

A woman posted disparaging remarks about her manager on her Facebook page and was fired shortly afterward. The employee sued and won, with the court stating that the online post was no different than talking at the water cooler. Employees have a right to talk about their employers according to the Federal Labor Laws, and states with employment-at-will laws do not necessarily have the right to arbitrarily fire-at-will for reasons that are not legal (Hananel 2010). While not necessarily deemed illegal, what are the potential implications of posting disparaging comments about one's employer on social media sites?

court-martialed and served 7 years in federal prison. Manning's information theft is one on the most publicized cases of communication technology abuses in recent memory. Manning has since been released from prison, due to Obama's grant of clemency, and now has transitioned and identifies as Chelsea Manning (Kube and O'Hara 2017).

Employee privacy and employer rights frequently clash. When employees use a company computer or device, the company will probably win a legal battle over disputed communication. When employees use their own computers or devices; however, protection of free speech will likely apply. An employee does not have a reasonable assumption of privacy when using work equipment, and the company has the right to block Internet sites. Firing people for abusing the Internet or using the Internet to go to inappropriate Internet sites is not unusual (Turri, Maniam, and Hynes 2008). Therefore, company e-mail systems should not be used for personal messages, and personal e-mails using a private e-mail address (Yahoo, Gmail, and so on) should only be sent and answered during breaks or lunchtimes and not during work hours.

Table 6.2 shows examples of proper uses and improper uses of communication technology usage.

Table 6.2 Proper and improper uses of communication technology

Uses of communication technology

Proper uses	Improper uses
1. Speed of transactions: Use technology for ease of business transactions for better customer service. There is timeliness in transaction-dependent business relationships, e.g., business contract negotiations, credit card, and loan applications.	1. Personal use: Do not abuse company technology and hardware by using it in any way that can be construed as improper. Managerial monitoring is legal; current laws allow companies to read employees' e-mails and monitor other communications employees produce using company property. The company does own the computers (Turri, Maniam, and Hynes 2008).
2. File storage capacity: Store large proprietary files only in locations that require layers of access and security for retrieval. Large files are easy to store, and electronic file copies reduce the need for stored hard-paper copies of files.	2. Visiting pornographic websites at work: Do not view sexually explicit websites using company property. Internet addiction and abuse of the Internet in the workplace (e.g., cyber sexual relationships, scandalous friendships, criminal abuses, and more) are common problems (Griffiths 2010).
3. Files sharing: Follow directives from the team leader or project manager as to the protocol for coordination of file sharing and production schedules. Large teams can collaborate on complex projects, including employees from any geographic location with Internet access, by sharing files via e-mail attachments, or other file downloads.	3. Fraud: Do not conduct your personal online business at work. Electronic information can be easily stolen and misused for crime, including swindling, money laundering, and terrorism (Choo 2009).
4. Research and data processing: Use free resources as a first step in information gathering and researching a topic. Search engines such as Google Scholar and Bing make it possible to gain access to and organize billions of pages of information from the Internet.	4. Memorializing coarse language: Do not put curse words, insults, or threats in writing. In divorce and bankruptcy proceedings and other highly emotionally charged business law cases, embarrassed clients have seen their obscene language become a part of the official written record (Schnelling 2009).
5. Government information: Use technology to access the plethora of information the U.S. government has provided access to online, for free! Access to government information and documents and filing essential documents is practical; e.g., filing income tax returns with the IRS or an Affirmative Action Plan with the Office of Federal Contract Compliance Programs.	5. Pilfering privileged information: Do not abuse or misuse other people's information by being careless with how you retrieve, store, and delete their information. Confidential records can be copied, distributed, and sold, which undermines consumer safety and protection (Choo 2008).

Conducting Technology-Assisted Meetings

One of the positive impacts of communication technology for internal business activity is its usefulness for planning and conducting meetings. More than 20 years ago, Munter (1992) provided some guidelines that remain relevant for conducting a business meeting (1) preparation, (2) participation, and (3) decision making and follow-up. All are crucial for conducting a meeting successfully, whether in person or virtually. Furthermore, knowing when you should and should not conduct a meeting is a skill that will help you preserve your reputation among your colleagues and peers. They will be more likely to participate in your meetings, if they know you call meetings only when they are absolutely essential.

Preparation

Before calling any business meeting, there should always be a valid reason to meet. People in business loathe having their time wasted. Therefore, it is good to know if a meeting should be called or if an alternative to a meeting would suffice. Drew (1994) suggests several reasons when you should conduct a meeting and reasons when you should not conduct a meeting, as summarized in in Table 6.3:

Table 6.3   Criteria for holding a meeting

Hold the meeting if you need to:	Do not hold the meeting when there is:
1. resolve conflicts 2. reach group consensus 3. identify problems or solve them 4. discuss sensitive information 5. solicit support 6. generate fresh ideas or concepts 7. report on a project's progress 8. demonstrate something project related	1. a lack of a clear objective 2. no need for group decision 3. a scheduled meeting but it is not needed 4. a lack of key personnel who can attend 5. a higher cost to holding the meeting than its benefit 6. no negative effect if the meeting is not held

Once you have decided that a meeting is necessary, you must prepare for the meeting. A crucial part of meeting preparation includes writing an agenda which requires that five questions be answered: Who should attend your meeting? What will be discussed and accomplished at your meeting?

When will the meeting take place? Where will the meeting take place—face-to-face or virtually? Why is the meeting essential or necessary? An illustration of answers to these questions is presented in Table 6.4, which is developed in preparation for a meeting of design engineers and a senior

Table 6.4   First meeting matrix for the Antonio's Bizarre project with a tentative outline

Things to consider as you plan your meeting	
Who should attend? Jennifer Jones, *senior design editor* (and meeting chairperson) Frank Mays, *senior engineer*; Fred Williams, *market analyst*; Rene Alexander, *web designer*; Mary Wells, *assistant web designer*	**Meeting time: 60 minutes maximum** Individual talk time: 25 minutes Brainstorming time: 15 minutes Group consensus time: 15 minutes New business time: 5 minutes
What will we discuss and accomplish? We will discuss the Antonio's Bizarre project's feasibility, image, and brand.	Jennifer Jones (5 minutes) Frank Mays (5 minutes) Fred Williams (5 minutes) Rene Alexander (5 minutes) Mary Wells (5 minutes)
When will we meet? January 10, 20, at 3:00 p.m. EST	Subject to confirmation from all.
Where will we meet? First floor conference room located in the New Drake Building	Meeting place will be confirmed 24 hours after the agenda is finalized.
Why are we meeting? There needs to be a group consensus and agreement on the feasibility of the new changes to the Antonio's Bizarre project.	Brainstorming discussion will require approximately 15 minutes. Consensus building will take approximately 15 minutes.
The tentative agenda outline you distribute should look something like this: 1. The meeting will be called to order at 3:00 p.m. EST in the conference room on the first floor in the New Drake Building. 2. Those tentatively present: Jennifer Jones (meeting chairperson), Frank Mays, Fred Williams, Rene Alexander, and Mary Wells. 3. Jennifer Jones (meeting chairperson), Frank Mays, Fred Williams, Rene Alexander, and Mary Wells each will spend 5 minutes sharing their ideas on the feasibility of the proposed communication technologies for Antonio's Bizarre project parameters and branding components (this will take 25 minutes). 4. The Antonio's Bizarre project team will brainstorm for 15 minutes to narrow the ideas most plausible for the integration of the proposed communication technologies on the ideas shared (this will take 15 minutes). 5. The project team will strive to reach a consensus on the ideas shared (this will take 15 minutes). 6. Any new business will be discussed for 5 minutes at most. 7. The meeting will be adjourned at 4:00 p.m. EST.	

design editor, Jennifer Jones. Answering the aforementioned questions will save you a lot of time as you plan.

People need to know that the meetings they attend are necessary, and what will be accomplished that otherwise could not be accomplished without a meeting; these are important whether the meeting is face-to-face or virtual. Be sure whenever possible that the length of the meeting is not more than 1 hour. Break the total time into allotments. Make sure that each person is aware that he or she will need to come prepared for the meeting by associating each name with a topic or allotment of time. Distribute the agenda, and give each person a 24-hour deadline to make suggested changes to it.

Finalize the agenda once everyone expected to attend has made comments, or after the 24-hour deadline has lapsed. When possible, plan your meeting at least 1 week in advance of the scheduled meeting time.

Finalize the agenda once the meeting time and location is reserved. In the event that situations change or the meeting place is unavailable, you might need to reschedule the meeting, but the agenda action items can stay the same.

Participation

The agenda action items become the meeting minutes. Taking the minutes for a meeting is the chairperson's responsibility, although this can be assigned to another member of the committee or team or to an administrative assistant. Meeting minutes are different from transcription notes. Only the key points of the discussion and the items agreed upon should be reflected in the meeting minutes. For example, people speak at a rate of 150 words per minute on average. A 60-minute meeting means that if all words were recorded, the minutes would be the size of a novella. Thus, a 60-minute meeting should result in about one page of minutes. Each of the action items on the agenda represents a line item in the meeting minutes. Record only the key points of the discussion and what points were agreed upon.

Ask questions directly to those who are not actively participating. For those persons who talk too much or dominate the discussion, politely remind them that they will have or have had their 5 minutes. Then, politely ask the person whose turn it is to speak. This encouragement may be especially needed for persons from cultures where speaking out of turn or being too forward is considered rude behavior. During brainstorming, it is the chairperson's responsibility to be sure that criticisms of ideas are avoided and that good ideas are being generated. When it is time to narrow the ideas, ask each person to write down his or her top two or three. Then, hear from each person as the group narrows the ideas. If necessary, use Robert's Rules of Order for deciding on issues. Using voting and majority rule is a good strategy for formal meetings.

Decision Making and Follow-Up

When it is necessary to make a decision, it can be done either by a secret ballot or by raising hands for a yea or nay vote. If it is a sensitive matter, it is probably best to use a secret ballot; if it is not sensitive, then raising hands tends to be faster. Meeting management software can be used in face-to-face and virtual meetings to facilitate the capture and presentation of ideas and anonymous voting.

Once something is decided, the person who will implement the idea will need to be told, and there needs to be a follow-up that the idea was actually put into action.

Conducting Multicultural Business Meetings

Most cultural differences occur because the things people hold dear, value, and believe are not universally accepted. Conducting a multicultural business meeting means that managers must deal effectively with the tensions caused by competing cultures. Managers must also anticipate and reasonably accommodate cultural sensitivities and expectations. Finally, managers will need to recognize and overcome barriers to communication spawned from language idioms, expressions that cannot be translated, and nonverbal behaviors and cues.

In order to manage tensions, speak more slowly than normal, but not louder than normal. Asking questions is a way to be sure that others understand you and you understand them. Be sure that all individuals express their views. Those from some cultures will not share information unless the leader asks for their ideas. Realize that in certain cultures it is rude to give someone credit individually and that it is only correct to credit the whole group. Language will always be a problem in intercultural meetings. Though English might be the official choice, remember that it may be a second or third language for some of the people in the meeting. Using visuals is important so that people can see and read as well as hear what is being said. Remember that meanings of words can be very confusing. A case in point is the expression *to table*. When we table something in the United States, it means we are putting it aside to take up at a later time. In England, *to table* means to take up the matter immediately. Take nothing for granted and ask lots of questions to clarify anything that does not seem clear.

Anticipating and accommodating cultural sensitivities means being aware that everyone is not like you. If you are a female, this may entail wearing concealing clothing. Or, if people eat with their fingers, you might resist requesting a fork and eat with your fingers as well. Learning to eat with chop sticks will impress your Asian counterparts. Respect customs that are important to members of other cultural groups. For instance, if you are working with Muslims, they will be praying five times during the day; and during Ramadan they will be fasting, so not eating in front of them would be considerate. Talk to people and ask them about their culture; most people enjoy educating others about their country and people. Most importantly, if you make a mistake apologize, and do not be afraid to laugh at yourself. Removing communication barriers means learning what the other culture expects. Asking questions of your counterpart will show an interest on your part and encourage the other person to ask questions of you.

Conducting Virtual Business Meetings

Virtual meetings save on travel time and expense and are becoming increasingly popular in global business organizations. To a large degree, virtual meetings are like face-to-face meetings; and therefore, should follow the guidelines previously discussed. Global teams, however, have all the usual communication challenges, plus there may be team members who have never met face-to-face, who are in different time zones, and for which the technology may not be equivalent. It is difficult to establish relationships through technology, so meetings will probably not flow as easily as they do when everyone is face-to-face in the same meeting room. As a leader of a virtual team, take extra time to greet the members as they join the meeting, using small talk and showing personal interest, much as you would in a live meeting. Remember when you are setting up meetings that holidays around the world are different, so have a calendar of each country handy as you plan. Additionally, consider the time zone differences. While there may be no one time that works well for everyone, alternate so that the same people will not consistently have to meet in the middle of the night or the wee hours of the morning.

Because attention is harder to keep during virtual meetings, ask all participants to set their phones on mute so they can hear but will not cause distraction with background noises or coughing. Use the whiteboard feature in your meeting management software to encourage all participants share ideas. Consider the use of webcams, so that everyone can have a face attached with the name. Be sure to take notes and send them to everyone to be sure they are complete and that everyone understands what was discussed and what actions need to be taken.

You may need to poll people to get them into the discussion. Some may feel that their English is not good enough or that their opinions are not important. Allow people to use the whiteboard and type responses if they feel more comfortable doing that. If individuals are from different layers within the company, you may need to level the playing field by emphasizing that everyone's ideas are important and critical to what is being discussed.

Virtual meetings do require more effort than face-to-face meetings, if they are to be successful. Many organizations provide virtual meeting rooms that attendees can use while engaged in a virtual meeting, complete with a computer that has a camera, as well as Wimba, Skype, or a similar application that allows participants to be seen and heard. Other screen-sharing technologies are available for hosting online meetings such as Cisco's Telepresence.

When people do not participate in discussion, they are only accepting information rather than exchanging it. If they have something to say, it should be shared with the entire group. Making people feel a part of a team is very important in virtual meetings.

Summary

A broad definition of communication technology is electronic systems used for communication between individuals or groups. We define *communication technology* narrowly because of its usage by business persons for business reasons as *any electronic system used by business persons that fosters improved communication in their goal achievements.*

Technology affords a wide array of opportunities for improving and enhancing communication, yet it is not without its pitfalls. People are making wide use of technology to impact their social exchanges, their consumer activities, and their employment endeavors. Businesses use technology to carry their marketing message and to communicate more effectively with employees and other stakeholders. Some general pitfalls of communication technology usage are that people seem to lose their sense of discretion when using mobile devices in public and personal and public safety can be compromised, as when driving or when a device containing sensitive information is lost or stolen. Some people using technology to engage in sexting, which can result in embarrassment and remorse. Cyber bullying can be used by people in the workforce as well as by people in the private sector to insult, belittle, or threaten others.

Technology can be assistive to business meetings, whether face-to-face or virtual. Three guidelines for conducting a business meeting include (1) preparation, (2) participation, and (3) decision making and follow-up. Multicultural and virtual meetings pose additional challenges. Conducting a multicultural business meeting means managers must deal with the tensions caused by competing cultures, anticipate and reasonably accommodate cultural sensitivities and expectations, and effectively remove communication barriers. Virtual meetings can save companies significant time and money by making it possible for people in different parts of the world to meet. Virtual teams must overcome the challenges of loss of personal contact, time differences, and technology insufficiencies to bring about favorable outcomes.

References

Chapter 1

Barnard, C.I. 1968. *The Functions of the Executive*. Cambridge, MA: Harvard University Press.

Bedeian, A.G., and D.A. Wren. 2001. "Most Influential Management Books of the 20th Century." *Organizational Dynamics* 29, no. 3, pp. 221–5.

Bell, R.L., and J.S. Martin. 2008. "The Promise of Managerial Communication as a Field of Research." *International Journal of Business and Public Administration* 5, no. 2, pp. 125–42.

Brownell, J. 1990. "Perceptions of Effective Listeners: A Management Study." *Journal of Business Communication* 27, no. 4, pp. 401–15.

Drucker, P.F. 1954. *The Practice of Management*. Burlington, MA: Elsevier Ltd, pp. 265–67.

Frankel, L.P, and K.L. Otazo. 1992. "Employee Coaching: The Way to Gain Commitment, Not Just Compliance." *Employment Relations Today* 19, no. 3, pp. 311–20.

Froschheiser, A.N. October 2008. "Communication, Communication, Communication: The Most Important Key to Success in Business Leadership." *Supervision Magazine* 69, no. 10, pp. 9–11.

Geneen, H., and A. Moscow. 1984. *Managing*. New York, NY: Doubleday.

Gibson, C.B., and J.L. Gibbs. 2006. "Unpacking the Concept of Virtuality: The Effects of Geographic Dispersion, Electronic Dependence, Dynamic Structure, and National Diversity on Team Innovation." *Administrative Science Quarterly* 51, no. 3, pp. 451–95.

Harcourt, J., V. Richerson, and M.J. Wattier. 1991. "A National Study of Managers' Assessment of Organizational Communication Quality." *Journal of Business Communication* 28, pp. 348–65.

Hellriegel, D., S.E. Jackson, and J.W. Slocum, Jr. 2007. *Managing: A Competency-Based Approach 11e*. Mason, OH: Thomson/South-Western.

Kanawattanachai, P., and Y. Yoo. December 2007. "The Impact of Knowledge Coordination on Virtual Team Performance Over Time." *MIS Quarterly* 31, no. 4, pp. 783–808.

Lawler, E.E., L.W. Porter, and A. Tennenbaum. December 1968. "Managers' Attitudes toward Interaction Episodes." *Journal of Applied Psychology* 52, no. 6, pp. 432–9.

Morreale, S.P., and P.M. Backlund. 2002. "Communication Curricula: History, Recommendations, and Resources." *Communication Education* 51, no. 1, pp. 2–18.

Morreale, S., R.B. Rubin, and E. Jones. 1998. *Speaking and Listening Competencies*. Washington, DC: The National Communication Association.

Ouchi, W. 1981. *Theory Z: How American Business Can Meet the Japanese Challenge*. Reading, MA: Addison-Wesley Publishing Company.

Shelby, A.N. 1993. "Organizational, Business, Management, and Corporate Communication: an Analysis of Boundaries and Relationships." *Journal of Business Communication* 30, no. 3, pp. 241–67.

Spangler, W.S., J.T. Kreulen, and J.F. Newswanger. 2006. "Machines in the Conversation: Detecting Themes and Trends in Informal Communication Streams." *IBM Systems Journal* 45, no. 4, pp. 785–99.

Taylor, H., G. Fieldman, and S. Lahlou. 2005. "The Impact of a Threatening E-Mail Reprimand on the Recipient's Blood Pressure." *Journal of Managerial Psychology* 20, no. 1, pp. 43–50.

Merriam-Webster. March 15, 2014. "Management." http://www.merriam-webster.com

Yarbrough, B.T. 2003. "Leading Groups and Teams." In *Managerial Communication Series*, ed. J.S. O'Rourke. 4th ed. Mason, OH: South-Western.

Zuboff, S. 1988. *In the Age of the Smart Machine: The Future of Work and Power*. New York, NY: Basic Books.

Chapter 2

"Ahmadinejad under fire for hugging Chavez's mother," March 12, 2013. *The Associated Press.* https://www.cbsnews.com/news/ahmadinejad-under-fire-for-hugging-chavezs-mother/, (accessed January 5, 2019).

Arnsparger, A. 2008. "4genr8tns: Succeeding with Colleagues, Cohorts, and Customers," *Generations at Work.* http://www.generationsatwork.com/4genr8tns-succeeding-with-colleagues-cohorts-customers/ (accessed January 5, 2019).

Chaney, L.H., and J.S. Martin. 2014. *Intercultural Business Communication.* 6th ed. Upper Saddle River, NJ: Prentice.

Desai, S.P., and V Lele. 2017. "Correlating internet, Social Networks and Workplace—a case of Generation Z Students." *Journal of Commerce & Management Thought* 8, no. 4, pp. 802–815.

Hall, E.T. 1966. *The Hidden Dimension.* New York, NY: Anchor Books.

Hershatter, A., and M. Epstein. June, 2010. "Millennials and the World of Work: An Organization and Management Perspective." *Journal of Business Psychology* 25, no. 2, pp. 211–23.

Holder, T. January 1996. "Women in Nontraditional Occupations: Information-Seeking During Organizational Entry." *Journal of Business Communication* 33, no.1, pp. 9–27.

Jenkins, J. 2008. "Strategies for Managing Talent in a Multigenerational Workforce." *Employment Relations Today* 34, no. 4, pp. 19–26.

Martin, J.M., B.E. Hamilton, M.J.K. Osterman, A.K. Driscoll, and M.S. Patrick Drake. 2018. "Birth: Final Data for 2016." *National Vital Statistics Report* 67, no 1, pp. 1–54.

Kosoff, M. January 31, 2016. "Dozens of Teenagers Told us What's Cool in 2016-These are Their Favorite (and Least Favorite) Apps." *Business Insider*, http://www.businessinsider.com/teens-favorite-apps-in-2016-2016-1 (accessed May 17, 2018).

Kyles, D. December 2005. "Managing Your Multigenerational Workforce." *Strategic Finance*, pp. 53–55.

London, M., H.H. Larsen, and L.N. Thisted. 1999. "Relationships Between Feedback and Self-Development." *Group and Organization Management* 24, pp. 5–27.

Macon, M., and J. Artley. 2009. "Can't We All Just Get along? A Review of the Challenges and Opportunities in a Multigenerational Workforce." *International Journal of Business Research* 9, no. 6, pp. 90–94.

Miller, D.L., and L. Karakowsky. 2005. "Gender Influences as an Impediment to Knowledge Sharing: When Men and Women Fail to Seek Peer Feedback." *Journal of Psychology* 139, no. 2, pp. 101–118.

Shannon, C., and W. Weaver. 1949. *The Mathematical Theory of Communication.* Urbana, IL: University of Illinois Press.

Snyder, L.G. 2010. "Communication Challenges: Strategies to Bridge the Generational Divide." Presentation at the 2010 Association for Business Communication Convention, Chicago, IL.

Weaver, W. 1949. "Recent Contributions to the Mathematical Theory of Communication." *Mathematical Theory of Communication* 1, pp. 1–16.

Chapter 3

Applebaum, S.H., D. Louis, D. Makarenko, J. Saluja, and S.K. Meleshko. 2013. "Participation in Decision Making: A Case Study of Job Satisfaction and Commitment" (Part three). *Industrial and Commercial Training* 45, no. 7, pp. 412–19.

Bell, R.L. 2009. "Dialing in to the Hidden Hierarchy: A Content Analysis of Culture Content in Popular Press Business Books." *Journal of Leadership, Accountability and Ethics* 7, no. 3, pp. 41–60.

Deal, T.E., and A.A. Kennedy. 1982. *Corporate Cultures: The Rites and Rituals of Corporate Life.* Boston, MA: Addison-Wesley Publishing Company.

Dent, S.M., and J.H. Krefft. 2004. *Powerhouse Partners: A Blueprint for Building Organizational Culture for Breakaway Results.* Mountain View, CA: Davies-Black Publishing.

Flannery, T.P, D.A. Hofrichter, and P.E. Platten. 1996. *People, Performance, and Pay: Dynamic Compensation for Changing Organizations.* New York, NY: The Free Press.

Gibb, J.R. 1961. "Defensive Communication." *Journal of Communication* 11, no. 3, pp. 141–48.

Johnson, J.D., W.A. Donohue, C.K. Atkin, and S. Johnson. 1994. "Differences between Formal and Informal Communication Channels." *Journal of Business Communication* 31, no. 2, pp. 111–22.

Katz, D., and R. Kahn. 1966. *The Social Psychology of Organizations.* New York, NY: Harper & Row Publishers.

Kotter, J.P, and J.L. Heskett. 1992. *Corporate Culture and Performance.* New York, NY: The Free Press.

Manzoni, J., and J. Barsoux. 2009. "The Interpersonal Side of Taking Charge." *Organizational Dynamics* 38, no. 2, pp. 106–16.

Rapert, M.I., A. Velliquette, and J.A. Garretson. 2002. "The Strategic Implementation Process Evoking Strategic Consensus through Communication." *Journal of Business Research 55,* pp. 301–310.

Rigsby, J.A., and G. Greco. 2003. *Mastering Strategy: Insights from the World's Greatest Leaders and Thinkers.* New York, NY: McGraw-Hill.

Robertson, E. 2003. "How to Use a Communication Climate Model." *Strategic Communication Management 7,* no. 2, pp. 28–32.

Schein, E.H. 1992. *Organizational Culture and Leadership.* 2nd ed. San Francisco, CA: Jossey-Bass Inc., Publishers.

Sherriton, J., and J.L. Stern. 1997. *Corporate Culture/Team Culture: Removing the Hidden Barriers to Team Success.* New York, NY: AMACOM.

Trompenaars, F., and C. Hampden-Turner. 1998. *Riding the Waves of Culture: Understanding Cultural Diversity in Global Business.* 2nd ed. New York, NY: McGraw Hill.

Vries, L. February 9, 2005. "The Rise & Fall of Carly Fiorina," *CBS.* http://www.cbsnews.com/stories/2005/02/09/scitech/pcanswer/main672809.shtml (accessed February 4, 2014).

Weick, K.E. 2001. *Making Sense of the Organization.* Hoboken, NJ: Wiley-Blackwell.

Chapter 4

Bell, R.L., W. Guyot, P.H. Martin, and R.J. Meier. 2011. "The Power of Religion, Unpbringing, Certification, and Profession to Predict Moral Choice." *Journal of Legal, Ethical, and Regulatory Issues* 14, no. 1, pp. 1–24.

Beu, D.S., M.R. Buckley, and M.G. Harvey. 2003. "Ethical Decision-Making: A Multidimensional Construct." *Business Ethics: A European Review* 12, no. 1, pp. 88–107.

Donaldson, T., and T.W. Dunfee. 1999. "When Ethics Travel: The Promise and Peril of Global Business Ethics." *California Management Review* 41, no. 4, pp. 45–63.

Eisenberg, E., and H. Goodall, Jr. 2001. *Organizational Communication: Balancing Creativity and Constraints.* 3rd ed. New York, NY: Bedford/St. Martins.

Feder, B.J. August 27, 2002. "WorldCom Messages Suggest a Silencing Effort," *The New York Times-Business Day.* http://query.nytimes.com/gst/fullpage.html?res =9F05E0D7113CF934A1575BC0A9649C8B63, (accessed April 17, 2013).

Feinberg, J. (ed.). 1996. *Reason and Responsibility: Readings in Some Basic Problems of Philosophy.* 9th ed. Belmont, CA: Wadsworth, pp. 639–52.

Johnson, C.E., T.L. Sellnow, M.W. Seeger, M. Barrett, and K.C. Hasbargen. 2004. "Blowing the Whistle on Fen-Phen." *Journal of Business Communication* 41, no. 4, pp. 350–69.

Kohlberg, L. 1969. "Stage and Sequence: The Cognitive-Developmental Approach to Socialization." In *Handbook of Socialization Theory and Research,* ed. S.A. Goslin. Chicago, IL: Rand McNally, pp. 347–480.

Kotlikoff, L.J., and S. Burns. 2012. *The Clash of Generations: Saving Ourselves, Our Kids, and Our Economy.* Cambridge, MA: The MIT Press.

Lehman, C., and D. Dufrene. 2015. *BCOM: Business Communication, 4LTR Press, Student Edition 6.* Boston, MA: Cengage Learning.

Lewicki, R.J., D.M. Saunders, and J.W. Minton. 2007. *Essentials of Negotiation.* 2nd ed. Homewood, IL: Irwin/McGraw-Hill Higher Education.

60 Minutes Overtime Staff. March 18, 2012. *"Whistle Blower Facing Foreclosure Wins $18 Million."* http://www.cbsnews.com/8301–504803_162–57397490-10391709/whistleblower-facing-foreclosure-wins-$18-million/, (accessed April 17, 2012).

Martin, J.M., B.E. Hamilton, M.J.K. Osterman, A.K. Driscoll, and P. Drake. 2018. "Birth: Final Data for 2016." *National Vital Statistics Report* 67, no. 1, pp. 1–54.

Taylor, K. April 10, 2018. "Teens Have a New Favorite Fast-Food Chain," *The Business Insider.* http://www.businessinsider.com/chick-fil-a-wins-over-teens-2018-4, (accessed May 16, 2018).

Trevino, L.K., and S.A. Youngblood. 1990. "Bad Apples in Bad Barrels: A Causal Analysis of Ethical Decision Making Behavior." *Journal of Applied Psychology* 75, no. 4, pp. 378–85.

U.S. Department of Justice. February 14, 2013. *"Former Executives of Stanford Financial Group Entities Sentenced to 20 Years in Prison for Roles in Fraud Scheme."* http://www.justice.gov/opa/pr/2013/february/13-crm-200.html, (accessed March 15, 2014).

Wikipedia. 2018. "Social Programs in the United States." https://en.wikipedia .org/wiki/Social_programs_in_the_United_States, (accessed May 16, 2018).

Zaremba, A. 2000. "Is Honesty Overrated: Employ Attitudes Toward Ethical Communication." *Journal of Employee Communication Management,* pp. 38–47.

Chapter 5

Bell, R.L. 2013. "Removing the Source of Conflict from Conflict Situations." *Supervision* 74, no. 11, pp. 3–4.

Casse, P., and Deol, S. 1991. *Managing Intercultural Negotiations: Guidelines for Trainers and Negotiators.* Washington, DC: Sietar International.

Cellich, C. July 1, 1997. "Communication Skills for Negotiations." *International Trade Forum* 3, pp. 22–28.

Chambers, M. 2009. "A Preliminary Hearing Is Not Enough: Tips for a Well-Managed Arbitration." *Dispute Resolution Journal* 64, no. 3, pp. 52–60.

Han, G., and P.D. Harms. 2010. "Team Identification, Trust and Conflict: A Mediation Model." *International Journal of Conflict Management* 21, no. 1, pp. 20–43.

Herzog, K. May 23, 2018. "After Evergreen: One Year Later, Bret Weinstein and Heather Heying Look Back," *The Stranger.* https://www.thestranger.com/features/2018/05/24/26472992/after-evergreen, (accessed September 2, 2018).

Kuhn, T. November, 1998. *Group Process and Group Performance: A Qualitative, Longitudinal Study of Conflict and Decision Making. Paper Presented at the 84th Annual Meeting of the National Communication Association,* New York, NY.

Kuhn, T., and M.S. Poole. 2000. "Do Conflict Management Styles Affect Group Decision Making?" *Human Communication Research* 26, no. 4, pp. 558–90.

Lichtash, A. 2004. "Inappropriate Use of E-Mail and the Internet in the Workplace: The Arbitration Picture." *Dispute Resolution Journal* 59, no. 1, pp. 26–36.

Maznevski, M., and H. Lane. 2004. "Shaping the Global Mindset: Designing Educational Experiences for Effective Global Thinking and Action." In *Teaching and Experiencing Cross-Cultural Management: Lessons from Master Teachers,* eds. N. Boyacigiller, R.M. Goodman, and M. Phillips. London, UK and New York, NY: Routledge.

Noll, D.E. 2009. "The Myth of the Mediator as Settlement Broker." *Dispute Resolution Journal* 64, no. 2, pp. 42–8.

Putnam, L.L., and C.E. Wilson. 1982. "Communicative Strategies in Organizational Conflicts: Reliability and Validity of a Measurement Scale." In *Communication Yearbook 6,* eds. M. Burgoon. Beverly Hills, CA: Sage, pp. 629–52.

Sillars A.L., S.F. Colletti, D. Parry, and M.A. Rogers. 1982. "Coding Verbal Conflict Tactics: Nonverbal and Verbal Correlates of the 'Avoidance-Distributive-Integrative' Distinction." *Human Communication Research* 9, pp. 83–95.

Smythe, J. 2007. "Employee Engagement—Its Real Essence." *Human Resource Management International Digest* 15, no. 7, pp. 11–13.

Stanley C.A., and N.E. Algert. 2007. "An Exploratory Study of the Conflict Management Styles of Department Heads in a Research University Setting." *Innovative Higher Education* 32, pp. 49–65.

Walton. R.E., and R.B. Mckersie. 1965. *A Behavioral Theory of Labor Negotiations: An Analysis of a Social Interaction System.* New York, NY: McGraw-Hill.

Chapter 6

Bailey, A., and D. Becker. November 21, 2016. "Mass. Professor's List of False, Misleading News Sites Goes," *Viral.* http://www.wbur.org/radioboston/2016/11/21/fake-news-tech, (accessed September 17, 2018).

Bell, R.L., W. Guyot, P.H. Martin, and R.J. Meier. 2011. "The Power of Religion, Upbringing, Certification, and Profession to Predict Moral Choice." *Journal of Legal, Ethical, and Regulatory* 14, no. 1, pp. 1–24.

Birkinshaw, J., and S. Crainer. Autumn, 2007. "e-Jamming." *Business Strategy Review* 18, no. 3, pp. 23–27.

Burke, K. August 4, 2015. "8 Reasons Why Texting is Crucial to Business Communication," *TEXT REQUEST.* https://www.textrequest.com/blog/reasons-why-texting-crucial-business-communication, (accessed September 19, 2018).

Choo, K. 2008. "Organised Crime Groups in Cyberspace: A Typology." *Trends in Organized Crime* 11, no. 3, pp. 270–95.

Choo, K. 2009. "Money Laundering and Terrorism Financing Risks of Prepaid Cards Instruments?" *Asian Journal of Criminology* 4, no. 1, pp. 11–30.

Drew, J. 1994. *Mastering Meetings: Discovering the Hidden Potential of Effective Business Meetings.* Toronto, Canada: McGraw-Hill Ryerson.

GHSA, Governors Highway Safety Association. 2018. "The State's Voice on Highway Safety." https://www.ghsa.org/state-laws/issues/Distracted-Driving, (accessed September 17, 2018).

Griffiths, M. 2010. "Internet Abuse and Internet Addiction in the Workplace." *Journal of Workplace Learning* 22, no. 7, pp. 463–72.

Guynn, J. June 27, 2018. "Google Gets Tough on Harassment After James Damore Firing Roils Staff." *USA Today.* https://www.usatoday.com/story/tech/news/2018/06/27/google-toughens-rule-internal-harassment-after-james-damore-firing-roils-staff/738483002/, (accessed September 17, 2018).

Hananel, S. November 10, 2010. "Feds: Woman Illegally Fired for Facebook Remarks," *The Commercial Appeal,* p. 1.

Kube, C. and M.E. O'Hara. May 17, 2017. "Chelsea Manning Released From Prison After Obama Grants Clemency," *NBC News.* https://www.nbcnews.com/feature/nbc-out/chelsea-manning-released-prison-after-obama-grants-clemency-n760616, (accessed September 17, 2018).

Lapowsky, I. November 15, 2016. "Here's How Facebook Actually Won Trump the Presidency," *Wired.* https://www.wired.com/2016/11/facebook-won-trump-election-not-just-fake-news/, (accessed September 17, 2018).

Munter, M. 1992. *Guide to Managerial Communication.* 3rd ed. Englewood Cliffs, NJ: Prentice Hall.

Schnelling, A. 2009. "Loose Lips Sink Ships (and Cases and Careers): Exercise Care in Communications." *American Bankruptcy Institute Journal* 6, no. 16, pp. 66–7.

Stark, J., J.H. Rumpel, R.J. Meier, and R.L. Bell. 2008. "Rural and Ethnic Young Consumers' Perceptions of Bundled Cellular Telephone Features." *Academy of Marketing Studies Journal* 12, no. 2, pp. 1–18.

Turri, A.M., B. Maniam, and G. Hynes. 2008. "Are They Watching? Corporate Surveillance of Employees' Technology Use." *The Business Review, Cambridge* 11, no. 2, pp. 126–30.

U.S. Department of Justice, Office of Justice Programs. July, 2013. "Electronic Communications Privacy Act of 1986 (ECPA), 18 U.S.C. § 2510-22," *Justice Information Sharing*, https://it.ojp.gov/default.aspx?area=privacy&page=1285, (accessed July 7, 2013).

Wallace, G. May 4, 2016. "The Anti-Trump Movement Spent Upwards of $75 million And Ultimately Lost," *CNN*. https://www.cnn.com/2016/05/04/politics/anti-donald-trump-movement-75-million-lost/index.html, (accessed September 17, 2018).

Zimdar, M. November 18, 2016. "My 'Fake News List' Went Viral. But Made-Up Stories Are Only Part of the Problem," *The Washington Post*. https://www.washingtonpost.com/posteverything/wp/2016/11/18/my-fake-news-list-went-viral-but-made-up-stories-are-only-part-of-the-problem/?utm_term=.a1c660e28ed0, (accessed September 17, 2018).

About the Authors

Reginald L. Bell is a professor of management in the College of Business at Prairie View A&M University. He received his PhD in business education from the University of Missouri at Columbia. He has several dozen articles published in peer-reviewed journals and proceedings and is a frequent contributor to *Supervision*. Bell serves as an ad hoc reviewer for the *International Journal of Business Communication* and the *Journal of Business and Technical Communication*; he serves on the editorial review board for the *Business and Professional Communication Quarterly*. His research has also appeared in the *Business and Professional Communication Quarterly, International Journal of Business Communication, Interdisciplinary Journal of E-Learning and Learning Objects, Journal of Applied Management and Entrepreneurship, Journal of Education for Business*, and *the Journal of Management Policy and Practice*.

Jeanette S. Martin is a professor emeritus in the School of Business at the University of Mississippi. She received her EdD in business education from the University of Memphis. She was previously a reviewer and associate editor for the *Journal of Business Communication* and reviewer for the *International Association of Intercultural Relations*. Her research has appeared in the *Journal of Education for Business, Journal of Business Communication, Management Communication Quarterly*, and others. She has published three books: *Global Business Etiquette, The Essential Guide to Business Etiquette, Passport to Success*, a chapter in *Handbook of Ethnic Conflict*, and a textbook *Intercultural Business Communication*.

Index

OTHER TITLES IN OUR CORPORATE COMMUNICATION COLLECTION

Debbie DuFrene, Stephen F. Austin State University, *Editor*

- *How to Write Brilliant Business Blogs, Volume I: The Skills and Techniques You Need* by Suzan St. Maur
- *How to Write Brilliant Business Blogs, Volume II: What to Write About* by Suzan St. Maur
- *Public Speaking Kaleidoscope* by Rakesh Godhwani
- *The Presentation Book for Senior Managers: An Essential Step by Step Guide to Structuring and Delivering Effective Speeches* by Jay Surti
- *Managerial Communication and the Brain: Applying Neuroscience to Leadership Practices* by Dirk Remley
- *Communicating to Lead and Motivate* by William C. Sharbrough
- *64 Surefire Strategies for Being Understood When Communicating with Co-Workers* by Walter St. John
- *Business Research Reporting* by Dorinda Clippinger
- *English Business Jargon and Slang: How to Use It and What It Really Means* by Suzan St. Maur
- *Conducting Business Across Borders: Effective Communication in English with Non-Native Speakers* by Adrian Wallwork
- *Strategic Thinking and Writing* by Michael Edmondson
- *Business Report Guides: Research Reports and Business Plans* by Dorinda Clippinger
- *Business Report Guides: Routine and Nonroutine Reports and Policies, Procedures, and Instructions* by Dorinda Clippinger
- *Managerial Communication For Professional Development* by Reginald L. Bell and Jeanette S. Martin

Announcing the Business Expert Press Digital Library

Concise e-books business students need for classroom and research

This book can also be purchased in an e-book collection by your library as

- *a one-time purchase,*
- *that is owned forever,*
- *allows for simultaneous readers,*
- *has no restrictions on printing, and*
- *can be downloaded as PDFs from within the library community.*

Our digital library collections are a great solution to beat the rising cost of textbooks. E-books can be loaded into their course management systems or onto students' e-book readers. The **Business Expert Press** digital libraries are very affordable, with no obligation to buy in future years. For more information, please visit **www.businessexpertpress.com/librarians**. To set up a trial in the United States, please email **sales@businessexpertpress.com**.

CPSIA information can be obtained
at www.ICGtesting.com
Printed in the USA
LVHW080809141221
705916LV00006B/123

9 781947 843318